FOREST BUDS,

FROM

THE WOODS OF MAINE.

BY

FLORENCE PERCY.

BOSTON:
BROWN, BAZIN & CO.
PORTLAND:
FRANCIS BLAKE.
1856.

Printed by Bazin & Chandler,
37 Cornhill, Boston.

TO ALL WHO LOVE ME.

Ye who have watched me since I chose
  The path which leads me here to-day,
Oft like a child who Maying goes,
  Tripping and stumbling on the way, —
Ye whose sweet words of love and trust
  Have cheered me when my faith was dim,
Till Hope rose smiling from the dust
  And sung anew her triumph-hymn, —
And ye whose hands in friendship true
  Have never yet been clasped in mine, —
One moment, while I bring to you
  The wreath which I have dared to twine.
No garland faint with rich perfumes
  To cloy the sense and charm the brain,
But simple buds and half-oped blooms
  Born in the rugged woods of Maine.

I know that 'mid the gorgeous flowers
  Which happier hands have culled away
From Poesy's enchanted bowers,
  The garland which I bring to-day
Is but a wreath of rugged stems
  Tied with a few imperfect blooms,
Beside the orange-groves' pure gems
  And the magnolia's rich perfumes,

I fling no rare exotics down,
  Brothers and sisters at your feet,
The dandelion's golden crown,
  The early snow-drop, low and sweet,
The buttercup with sultry hue,
  The wild-rose sought by dainty bees,
Rich clover-blooms and violets blue,
  And the pink snow of orchard-trees
Are here; — the arbutus that hides
  Among dead leaves and sprouting brakes, —
Sweet nameless flowers from river-sides
  And lilies from our northern lakes.

And as a traveller far away
  From northern scenes and northern loves,
Grows faint with breathing day by day
  The fragrant breath of spicy groves —
Grows tired of blossoms rich and bright,
  Such as a tropic summer knows,
And welcomes with a deep delight
  The perfume of a sweet home-rose, —
Or pained by the bewildering songs
  Of eastern birds with gorgeous wings,
Turns wearily away and longs
  To hear the strain our robin sings,
Mayhap some hearts will turn away
  From songs more lofty and divine,
And tired of a sublimer lay
  Will listen for a while to mine.

CONTENTS.

ADA.

HERS is one of those sweet faces
Made to light earth's darkest places, —
Wherein childhood's playful archness brightens earnest thought's repose, —
She is fairer, purer, sweeter,
Than when woman's years shall greet her,
Even as is the bud unblossomed sweeter than the ripened rose.

There is no voluptuous splendor
In her face so pure, so tender, —
Naught of mid-summer perfection, — 't is the promise of young June, —
Naught of womanhood's completeness, —
But an innocence, a sweetness
Dearer far, as is the morning lovelier than the perfect noon.

Less an angel, — more a woman, —
Less etherial and more human
Will she be when five more Aprils shall have browned each sunny curl, —
She will seem another creature,
Changed in heart and hope and feature,
When the *woman's* cares and trials drown the visions of the *girl.*

Lapsed in bright and gorgeous dreaming
With romance's rose-rays gleaming,
Yet she makes a gentle effort to awaken from its power,
Conscious of a sphere of being
Just beyond her tinted seeing,
Like a bee at morning drowsing in a yet unopened flower.

And she looks with childish wonder
Toward the misty realm beyond her,
Where are cares and strifes and discords, — toil for heart and hand and brain, —
But she hearkens all unfearing
Like a young bird faintly hearing
From beneath its mother's pinions, the rude rushing of the rain.

Time will be no partial preacher, —
Good and evil he will teach her —
Hopes and fears will fill her bosom, — joys and griefs will try their power,

But the innocency tender
Haloing her brow with splendor,
Will depart, as does the rain-drop from the forehead of a
flower.

As a woman she is fated, —
She will be adored, and hated, —
Know all depths of joy and sorrow, — see glad days and
gloomy years; —
And her path that now lies glowing
Through green vales, — by streams sweet flowing,
Will wind sadly through dark places, where the ground is
wet with tears.

Ah, the "evil days" are nearing,
When her day-dreams disappearing,
She will wake to mourn the absence of this freshness, joy,
and truth,
And her spirit backward turning
Will be vaguely, vainly yearning
For the tender light and gladness of the Morning Land of
youth.

Ah, that woman's gladdest laughter
Has a mournful echo after!
Ah, that time should sow wild discord 'mid her heart's
resounding strings!

Ah, that wealth and pride and power
Should eclipse love's holy dower,—
That earth's soiling dust should gather on her spirit's snowy wings!

Stay awhile, oh, dawning maiden!
Coming time with change is laden,—
Linger yet upon the threshold of thy womanhood's domain;—
For as years around thee cluster,
Though they bring thee added lustre,
They will take a bloom, a freshness, that will never come again!

MAY.

THE lingering hours of the winter
  Have dragged themselves wearily by,
And my spirit springs up, like a wild-bird,
  To the first summer-blue of the sky.

The dark forests stand in the sunshine
  Like armies on mountain and plain,
And o'er their brown ranks, the sweet spring-time
  Unfurls her green banner again.

Since the first ruddy blush of the morning
  Broke over the hill-tops afar,
Till now, when the dim earth is sleeping
  In the light of the evening star.

I have wandered alone through the forest,
  To listen its murmuring song,
And watch the young leaf-buds awaking
  From their slumbers so dreamless and long.

But methought it seemed cheerless and dreary
Till, brushing the dead leaves apart,
I found the sweet May-flowers springing
Like hope in a desolate heart.

I sat, as of old, by the brook-side,
Where clouds of blue violets lie
In beauty along the green hollows,
Like fragments dropt down from the sky, —

But my heart was o'erburdened with sadness,
For I missed the dear hand that of yore
I clasped in my own as I wandered, —
Alas, I shall clasp it no more!

There was one to the charm of whose presence
My spirit adoringly bowed,
And the light of her love shone around me,
Like sunshine encircling a cloud.

When last the sweet season of May-time
Was mingling its smiles with its showers,
I wandered with her in the woodland,
And hunted with her for the flowers.

Oh, her step was as light as the dew-fall,
And her voice like a bird's in the skies,
And the light of a glad loving spirit
Shone soft in her sunny brown eyes.

The dead leaves lie damp in the grave-yard
  Where sadly last autumn they fell.
And under them sleeps, oh, how sweetly.
  The dear one who loved me so well.

For since the last summer-time's flowers
  Grew pale at the kiss of the frost.
She has sung the sweet songs of the angels,
  And I, — I have mourned her as lost.

And now, when I thread the dark wood-paths.
  Which once she delighted to trace.
My heart sinks down heavy and voiceless,
  For I meet not her beautiful face.

But though my dim eyes see not clearly.
  Yet oft o'er my sorrow is thrown
The bliss of her glorified presence.
  And I feel that I am not alone.

I LOVE THEE.

I love thee!
Not for thy glorious eye's unrivalled brightness, —
Not for the gentle grace thy features wear,
Not for thy marble brow's unsullied whiteness,
Not for the shining ripples of thy hair, —
Not for thy lips, like rosebuds half unfolded,
Not for thy flute-like voice's silver tone,
Not for thy rounded form, in beauty moulded, —
Nay, not for these I love thee, dearest one!

For the warm love-light in thy dark eye shining,
For the strange charm that makes thy presence bliss,
For thy pure soul, a lofty faith enshrining,
For thy true heart of trusting tenderness, —
For thy kind words, which cheer the stricken-hearted,
For thy bright smile, the same through good and ill,
For the low prayer that blessed me when we parted,
For the sweet hope that glads my spirit still,
I love thee!

BY THE RIVER-SIDE.

Down by the river-side sat I alone,
Hearing the waters' low musical moan,
Waiting the while for a tarrying boat, —
Hark, to the mariner's echoing note!

Fair was the boatman as eye may behold,
How the breeze lifted his tresses of gold!
While o'er his shoulders so dimpled and white
Lay his soft wings, half unfolded for flight.

Smoothly the shining waves bore him along,
And, at each pause in his magical song,
Lightly he leaned from the boat's dipping side,
Pulling the lilies afloat on the tide.

Gazing I stood on the wave-beaten shore,
Counting by heart-throbs the sweeps of his oar, —
Murmuring, "Boatman, come hither to me,
I would float over the waters with thee!"

Upright he sprang as he heard my low call,
Quickly the buds from his fingers let fall,
And with a motion obedient and fleet,
Softly the boat glided up to my feet.

Lightly I swung from an o'er-sweeping vine,
Half-clasped the fingers extended to mine,
When with light laughter, eluding my hand,
Pushed he the shallop away from the land,

And, with a sweep of the fairy-like oar,
Floated away by the opposite shore, —
While his sweet voice floated back on the wind,
"Have ye heard never the boatman is blind?"

Down the bright stream, like a vision of light,
Glided the boatman with wings gleaming white,
And as away sped the fair little craft,
Heard ye how gaily the mariner laughed?

Lonely and sad on the shore I sat down,
Twisting the willow leaves into a crown,
Catching at times the sweet chorus of joy
Borne from the lips of the beautiful boy.

Thus do I wait on life's wave-beaten beach,
Longing for blessings I never may reach, —
Seeing all gladsome and beautiful things
Pass from my gaze, like the gleam of his wings.

Vanished forever! yet deep in my heart
Still of his presence there lingers a part,
For as his bark idly floated along,
Learned I the notes of his wildering song.

Pass on, bright visions, and vanish from sight,
Tearless I gaze, for I mourn not your flight, —
Though on the shore I wait lonely and long,
If I may cheat the dull moments with song!

A JUNE SHOWER.

How this delicious rain
Brings up the flowers! One might almost say
It rains down blossoms, — for where yesterday
I sought for them in vain,
They lie by thousands on the wet green earth,
Rejoicing in the freshness of their birth.

No harsh or jarring sound
Breaks the refreshing stillness of the hour, —
The tinkling foot-falls of the passing shower
Patter along the ground, —
The swallows twitter gladly from the eaves,
And the small rain talks softly to the leaves.

Bloom-laden lilac trees,
Their purple glories dripping with the rain,
Shake off the drops in odorous showers again, —
And the small fragrances
Of cherry-blossoms, and of violets blue,
Come balmily the open window through.

With idly-folded hands
The farmer sits within his cottage door,
Watching the blessings which the full clouds pour
Upon his thirsty lands,—
Where written promise by his eye is seen
In visible characters of living green.

Unyoked the oxen stand,
The cool rain plashing on their heaving sides,
And with wide nostrils breathe the fragrant tides
Of breezes flowing bland,—
Then as though sated with the odor sweet,
Crop the new grass that springs beneath their feet.

Sweet is the gladsome song
Which the young birds sing in the summer time,
The wind's soft voice, the river's wavy chime
Flowing in joy along,—
But dearer far to me the pleasant tune
Sung by the rain-drops in the month of June.

DROWNED.

Pale and drooping as a bruiséd lily
Lies he 'mid the river-grasses chilly,
Like a fragile zephyr-wafted blossom
Rocked to rest upon the river's bosom.

Raise him gently from the tangled rushes;
No soft life-glow now his pale face flushes,
And his lip's warm hue is quenched forever,
By the envious kisses of the river.

Part the wet curls from his marble forehead,
Which so soon death's icy chill hath borrowed,—
Let the little hands, so smoothly moulded,
Softly on the quiet breast be folded.

Press the waxen lids serenely over
The blue orbs they seem so loth to cover,—
Lay around the fair face, cold and pearly,
Fragile buds, and blooms that perish early.

Let no tear-drops on your lashes glisten, —
With faith's steady strength look up and listen; —
Hear ye not the songs of the immortals
Welcoming his soul to glory's portals?

With soft steps and hearts subdued and lowly,
Leave him to his slumbers pure and holy,
Weep not over heart-strings crushed and riven,
Mourn not for a soul flown home to heaven!

THE ANGEL OF PATIENCE.

Beside the toilsome way
Lonely and dark, by fruits and flowers unblest,
Which my worn feet tread sadly, day by day,
Longing in vain for rest.

An angel softly walks,
With pale sweet face, and eyes cast meekly down,
The while from withered leaves and flowerless stalks
She weaves my fitting crown.

A sweet and patient grace,
A look of firm endurance, true and tried,
Of suffering meekly borne, rests on her face
So pure — so glorified.

And when my fainting heart
Desponds and murmurs at its adverse fate,
Then quietly the angel's bright lips part,
Murmuring softly, "Wait!

'Patience!' she sweetly saith, —
The Father's mercies never come too late;
Gird thee with patient strength and trusting faith,
And firm endurance, — wait!"

Angel! behold, I wait,
Wearing the thorny crown through all life's hours, —
Wait till thy hand shall ope the eternal gate,
And change the thorns to flowers!

THE FOREST.

In my childhood's April days,
 Ere I learned life's deeper meaning,—
When I walked in pleasant ways,
 Flowers amid the brambles gleaning,—
While unspoiled by frost or blight
 Was my heart's unshadowed centre,
And its fulness of delight
 Left no room for grief to enter,—
When earth seemed a blissful clime,
 Full of joy and pleasant duty,
And my pulse was beating time
 To the songs of love and beauty,—
Fanciful—companionless,
 Heart and brain with visions teeming—
Solitude and loneliness
 Taught to me the art of dreaming.

Many a bright imagining,
 Many a fair prophetic vision
Came on fancy's tireless wing,
 Clad in hues almost elysian.

And my favorite dreaming-place
  Was an old and shadowy forest;—
Oh, how oft in later days,
  When my heart is throbbing sorest,
And life's burning desert-sand
  Painfully my worn feet parches,
Think I of that fairy land,
  With its cool and winding arches,
In the deep and fragrant shade
  All unbrokenly enfolden,
Save when sportive winds which played
  'Mid the forest monarchs olden,
Did the yielding branches woo
  To and fro with gentle power,
And the sun-rays drifted through
  In a dazzling golden shower.

Seldom by a human sound
  Was the wood's deep quiet broken,
And the solitude profound
  Gave of human life no token.
Nature, sabbath-like and calm
  Smiling at her own completeness,
Breathing quietude and balm,
  Sleeping in a trance of sweetness,
Did a mystic charm impart
  To the dim and shadowy pleasance,
Seeming to my childish heart
  Like a high majestic presence.

Very lovely was the wood
  At the summer's early coming,
When the breathing solitude
  Was one sweet and ceaseless humming;—
Then the maples, gnarled and old,
  Veiled in moss, like ancient castles,
Did their rugged limbs enfold
  In a robe of crimson tassels;—
Then a warmer, sunnier hue
  Mingled with the pine's dark fringes,
And the green buds melted through
  The dark hemlock's sombre tinges;
Then the willow's bending stems
  Were with downy blossoms sprinkled,
And the winter-green's bright gems
  In the bright leaves smiled and twinkled;
Then the snow-drop sought to hide,
  Whence the winds their fragrance borrowed,
Like a young and bashful bride
  With bright dew-pearls on her forehead;
And the timid violet
  Sprang amid the mosses tender,
With its cup all dewy wet
  Drooping on its stem so slender,—
Like a heart bereft of cheer,
  O'er some hidden sorrow pining,
Smiling, even while a tear
  In its veiléd depths enshrining.

Birds there were, a countless throng
  Making in the wood their dwelling,
Breaking into fitful song
  Tales of love and gladness telling;
There the joyous wood-lark sprung
  From his nest, at morning's breaking,
Drops of dew, like pearls unstrung,
  From his trembling pinions shaking,
And amid the birch-tree tops
  Swinging, warbled, all a-quiver,
Notes like ringing shower-drops
  On the bosom of a river;
Then the cuckoo timidly
  Hidden in some lofty hollow,
Wove its sweet monotony
  With the chirping of the swallow, —
And the bright-winged goldfinch came
  Darting from the reedy meadows,
Glancing like a jet of flame,
  In and out among the shadows, —
And the robin's merry song
  Loud and mellow and sonōrous,
Echoed cheerily along
  Mingling with the general chorus, —
With a throng of nameless birds,
  Whose brief songs, abruptly ending,
Came like sweetly spoken words
  In the pauses softly blending.

And when morning woke the earth
From its dim and quiet sleeping,
Then a strain of joy and mirth
From the wood went upward sweeping.
Scores of birds, the trees among,
Where the sun's first ray was burning,
Bursting into happy song,
Welcoming the day's returning,
Kept the echoes ringing round,
In a dance of tinkling changes,
As a wind-harp's varying sound
O'er the diapason ranges.

When the autumn's veil of mist,
O'er the earth was wide enfolden,
And the subtle alchemist
Changed the emerald leaves to golden,—
Then before the raptured eye
Shone a scene of wondrous splendor,
Matching even the rainbow's dye
With its hues so rich and tender;—
Though the daintiest blossoms drooped
At the autumn's chill advancing,
Still amid the dark leaves grouped
Were the clustered berries glancing,—
And the rugged autumn flowers
With their cheerful hardy faces,
Came like smiles in lonely hours,
Lighting up the gloomiest places.

Often in the autumn eves
  To the wood my footsteps wandered,
And amid the falling leaves
  Silent, sat I down and pondered
With a kind of childish awe
  On the beauty round me beaming,
Till the night began to draw
  Her dark curtains round my dreaming;
Or where danced the brook along
  With a sound like childish laughter,
With an answering laugh and song,
  I went gaily dancing after;
Pausing oft upon its brink,
  Where the wild grapes gleamed most brightly,
And pale asters knelt to drink,
  Kissing the cool waters lightly, —
Weaving garlands long and bright
  Of the leaves around me straying,
Or in childhood's gay delight
  With the shining pebbles playing.

Glimpses of the days to be,
  Dreams of happiness and glory
Wove their bright spells over me
  In that forest wild and hoary; —
And the sad mysterious sound
  Which the wind was ever making
'Mid the swaying boughs around
  Mournful echoings awaking,

In the distance, lone and drear,
  With a solemn cadence sighing,
Fell upon my listening ear
  Like a voice of prophecying;—
Though these dreamings fled away,
  Fled with childhood's dim sweet morning,
Yet I think of them alway
  As a sweet and slighted warning.

Thus, through all the genial hours,
  While the wild brook frolicked gaily,
Through the forest's sylvan bowers
  Went I to its margin daily,—
Till the autumn days grew brief,
  And the lonesome winds were wailing,
And the last sere blighted leaf
  From the lightened bough was sailing,—
Till the snow in sudden wrath,
  Heralding the boisterous comer,
Quite obscured the little path
  Worn so smoothly all the summer;—
And when freezing snow-drifts lay
  Coldly on the earth's chill bosom,
Seemed to me that still alway
  In the wood were bud and blossom,—
And that though the loud winds rung
  Fiercely over vale and meadows,
Still the summer warblers sung
  In the forest's fragrant shadows.

Those sweet days are with the past, —
  Gone — whence there is no returning,
Yet with glances backward cast
  Oft I find my spirit yearning
For those murmuring forest shades
  Loved in long-ago existence,
Where the lofty cool arcades
  Lost themselves in leafy distance.

I have wandered far since then,
  Led by fate, or called by duty,
But I ne'er have looked again
  On such scenes of wondrous beauty; —
Never since has note of bird
  In the woodland or the meadows
Charmed me like the songs I heard
  In the forest's whispering shadows;
Never more will flowers bloom
  Half so brightly to my seeing,
Never yield so sweet perfume
  As the ones which there had being.

Often since my cup of life, —
  Robbed of its first sparkling glitter
By reality and strife, —
  Has grown sadly dark and bitter,
Come the thoughts of those sweet hours
  Spent by joy and I together,
Like the memory of flowers
  In the frigid winter weather.

THE SPRING BY THE CHERRY TREE.

I LOVE to dream of the pleasant dell
  Where my childhood's gladsome hours were spent,
That flowery nook recalled so well
  With childish thoughts so deeply blent, —
The beautiful stream I used to love,
  Where the waters gushed so cool and clear, —
The shaded glen in the aspen grove,
  To gentle memory still more dear, —
Yet, musing dreamily, I think
  The happiest hours of life to me,
Were spent by the bright and mossy brink
  Of the crystal spring by the cherry tree.

Aside from the smoothly trodden way
  That I bounded o'er, on my way to school,
A deep, dark, forest-like dingle lay,
  Silent and shadowy and cool, —
And there in a dell like an emerald cup,
  A vine-hung, blossom-scented nook,

A beautiful spring gushed purely up,
  The source of a merrily laughing brook; —
A gnarled old cherry-tree's heavy bough
  Drooped o'er it with leaves of shining green, —
Methinks I can almost see them now,
  With the sunbeams sifting down between!

'T was there I gathered the eglantine,
  Its fragrance flooding the heavy air,
And the delicate stems of the celandine,
  With its gem-like flowers so brightly fair; —
And playfully shook from the honied cells,
  The drowsy bees which were humming there,
Then weaving in wreaths the golden bells
  Laughingly twisted them in my hair;
And there the beautiful violets grew,
  With fragrant breath and varying dyes, —
How fondly I likened their gentle blue
  To the hue of my mother's loving eyes!

Ah, often I've stood by that cool, deep spring
  Till my bare feet sunk in the yielding moss,
And watched on the surface, the glimmering
  Of the broken light as it flashed across; —
Or gazed far down to the circling rocks,
  Where the sparkling pebbles would glance and shine,
And a glad face shaded by golden locks,
  Was roguishly peeping up at mine, —

Oh, I almost doubt, as I sadly trace
The changes which time has wrought in me,
That mine is the same bright happy face
That shone in the spring by the cherry-tree!

For now could I gaze, as in days of yore,
In the answering depths of that limpid wave,
Alas! it would give me back no more
The pleasant picture that then it gave;—
The fearless gladness that childhood wears
Would shine no more on the sunny brow,
For the cares and sorrows of darker years
Have shadowed its careless brightness now;
And never again will my mirrored face
Beam half so brightly and joyously,
As the laughing one I was wont to trace
In the crystal spring by the cherry-tree!

FLOWN.

A beautiful birdling made its nest
In my dark and lonely heart,
And I fondly cherished my welcome guest,
And prayed with a grateful soul, and blest,
That always thus it might sweetly rest,
And never more depart.

I gazed in the soft bewildering deeps
Of its young unshadowed eyes, —
They were calm as the wave where a sunbeam sleeps, —
They were pure as the dew that the lily weeps,
And bright as the brightest star which keeps
Its watch in the midnight skies.

Its gushing voice was as sweet and clear
As the lays of seraphs blest; —
In melody on my raptured ear
It fell, like songs from a holier sphere,
With a wondrous power to soothe and cheer
My spirit's wild unrest.

And I watched above it with fond delight,
Till once on a quiet even,
It spread its beautiful wings in flight
And floated away from my longing sight,
Slow melting into the distance bright
Like a star in the morning heaven.

From the first sweet song of the early lark,
Till now, when on hill and plain,
The shadows of night fall dim and dark,
I have waited, its homeward flight to mark,
But the dove gone forth from my heart's lone ark,
Returneth not again.

And now I listen, alas, in vain,
Through the sad and cheerless hours,
For the clear wild notes of its gushing strain
To fall on my waiting ear again,
As the grateful drops of the summer rain
On the faint and drooping flowers.

No longer it gladdens my weary breast,
As in happy days of yore,
Or soothes my soul to a quiet rest
With its thrilling music, so sweet and blest, —
For the bird gone forth from my heart's warm nest,
Returns, alas, no more!

THE ANSWERED PRAYER.

A MAIDEN knelt in her chamber
  At the quiet close of day,
And prayed for her absent lover
  On the dark blue sea away.

She prayed for his safe returning,
  So vainly looked for yet, —
"Oh, grant," she said, "I may meet him
  Ere the morrow's sun shall set!"

The stormy night shut darkly
  Afar o'er the raging sea,
Where the bark of the absent lover
  Lay drifting hopelessly.

The angrily dashing billows
  Called loudly to the sky,
And the wind-god, fiercely raving,
  Howled back a harsh reply.

And, bravest of all the seamen,
  Was seen that lover's form,
Till the wrecked dismantled vessel
  Went down in the raging storm.

The maiden stirred in her slumbers,
  And whispered murmuringly,
While a smile passed over her features, —
  "Dearest, I come to thee!"

The beams of the rising morning
  O'er the tranquil ocean swept,
But deep in its quiet bosom
  The pale-browed lover slept.

At the maiden's vine-wreathed lattice
  Came in the rosy light,
But it fell on a pulseless bosom,
  And a face all still and white.

Why lieth the gentle maiden
  So silently cold and fair?
The Father, in love and mercy,
  Hath granted her evening prayer!

WINTER.

'Tis the bright and joyous season,
Ever fraught with glee and mirth,
Bringing happiness and plenty
To the glad and grateful earth,
And a ring of loving faces round the warm and sparkling hearth.

And the long bright winter evening
Passes merrily away,
While the quaint and varying shadows
On the ceiling dance and play,
And each radiant face grows brighter in the fire-light's rosy ray.

But my heart hath known no gladness
Since the autumn's breezy hours,
With their chill resistless breathing,
Swept the bloom from summer's bowers,
And the frost as coldly gathered on my heart as on the flowers.

For my spirit sadly muses
  On the loved and early lost,
On the many hopes and wishes
  By despair all coldly crossed,
Vanished now, alas! forever, — nipt like blossoms in a frost!

And the shrine where first and freshest
  Were my wrecked affections strown,
Is a lone deserted grave-yard,
  Where, when autumn leaves were brown,
She, the star of my existence, from my heart went coldly down!

Griefs that bind no more *her* spirit,
  Closely still my own enslave, —
Wilder storms than beat above her
  In my bosom darkly rave,
And the chilling snow-drifts deepen on my heart as on her grave.

For alas! the flowerless summer
  Of my blighted life is o'er,
And though spring to earth's cold bosom
  Will the bud and bloom restore,
Well I know the spring will brighten in my frozen heart no more.

As the lone and weary watcher
Counts the minutes' lingering flight,
With a patient, hopeful spirit
Waiting for the tarrying light,
Cheating thus the dreary hours of the long and lonesome night, —

So do I look gladly forward
Through the darkness of my way,
To where griefs and cares and trials
All, shall vanish in the ray
Of the spirit's heavenly dawning, — of the soul's unclouded day!

FROST-PICTURES.

THE frost-king hath clad the forest
In a garb of icy mail,
And left on the panes of the windows,
A white translucent veil.

Oh, a rare and radiant pencil
And a skilful hand hath he,
And none may mock or rival
His magical imagery.

Come hither ye sweet-voiced prattlers,
Who mourn for the summer lost, —
Come hither and see what beauties
Are born of the winter's frost.

'T is a scene in the northern regions,
Where through the lingering night,
The mystical borealis
Is lending its waving light.

Where the sledge and the fleet-paced reindeer
O'er the glittering snow-paths go,
And the bending boughs of the fir-trees
Are heavy with clinging snow.

Where the woods flash back the sunshine
From their load of glistening gems,
And clusters of glancing crystals
Depend from the swaying stems.

And afar in the frigid distance,
The glaciers crash and fall,
And ranks of towering icebergs
Form a strong and massive wall.

But the wayward painter wearied
Of his first imagining,
And bordered his wintry landscape
With the leaves and flowers of spring.

Alas, for the radiant picture
So truly and brightly drawn,
One smile of the winter sunshine
Hath touched it, and it is gone.

As fade, in our after being
The fancies and hopes of youth,
Or as vanish the shades of error
In the dawning light of truth.

No trace of the beauteous picture
On the weeping pane appears,
But mountain and plain and forest
Have melted in lucid tears.

Thus ever our blissful dreamings
Of the bright and blessed ideal,
Are scattered in tears and sadness
By the stern, remorseless real!

NO MORE.

When life has sailed far down time's darkening stream,
And silvery threads amid brown tresses gleam,
'T is mournful to know the heart's summer-time o'er,
And that never a blossom will bloom in it more.

But 't is sadder to know, at youth's bright morning hour,
Ere the sun-rays have kissed the fresh dew from the flower,
That love, hope and gladness are meaningless words,
And that life must henceforth be like June without birds!

THE HOUSEHOLD SAINT.

Thou whose sweet presence is with me now,
Thou whose light breathing fans my brow, —
  As drifts my hearts's dismantled ark
  O'er life's wide ocean, so dim and dark,
Thou, oh, thou art the white-winged dove
Bringing the olive-leaves of love!

Thine, my own, is the only eye
That never hath looked on me carelessly, —
  Thine are the only lips, my bird,
  Which have given me never an unkind word,
And thine is the only heart, which still
Loves on, unchanging, through good and ill.

Never upon thy beaming face
Has passion or sorrow left its trace,
  Never a shadow of sin or care
  Dimmed the light on thy forehead fair,
For thou art as pure and from guile as free
As the shining ones who wait for thee!

Words of the tempter I cannot hear,
While thy sweet love-tones charm my ear,
  Only prayers from my heart arise,
  When I gaze in thy holy eyes,
For all things dark and sinful flee
From the presence of truth and purity.

While I can clasp thy angel form
I can meet unshrinking, life's wildest storm,
  While I can hold thy tiny hand,
  Can every trial and woe withstand,
And walk at last, with untrembling breath,
Through the shadowy valley we know as death!

THIS MORNING.

Morning comes, and with rosy fingers
  Parting her misty locks away,
Binds them back with a golden arrow,—
  Then like a laughing child at play,
Waving the folds of her radiant garments,
  Sweeps the stars from the path of day.

Thou of the broad and thoughtful forehead,
  Over the calm reflective eyes,
Shrining a deep unworldly meaning
  Under the shadow that in them lies,
Let us forget life's jar and discord,
  Listening to Nature's harmonies.

Let us go where the bending branches
  Closest, coolest together press,
Where the leaves with their loving fingers
  Touch my forehead in mute caress—
Come, for the heart that loads my bosom
  Aches with its heavy emptiness.

Lightly the plumes of cherry-blossoms
  Drop their snow as we wander by,
Sweetly the bright waves talk together,
  Sweetly the willow boughs reply,
Fringing the brink of the smiling river
  As lashes shadow a clear blue eye.

Softly the elm's low drooping tresses
  Swing and wave, by the south-wind stirred,
Lightly the birch-tree's airy branches
  Tremble under the singing bird;
Sweetly the river's dreamy murmur
  Comes like an oft-repeated word.

Weary of worldly care and bustle,
  Oh, I deem it a blessed boon
Thus to rest where the rippling water
  Singeth ever a lulling tune,
While with its soft continuous murmur
  Mingle the myriad songs of June.

YESTERDAY.

An angel passed me yesterday,
  With snowy wings and floating hair,
As slowly on my devious way
  I went, in darkness and despair.

Strange how my heart could be so cold
  When that sweet angel-face was nigh!
I might have caught her robe's light fold
  As airly it floated by, —

I might have kissed the sun-bright flow
  Of curls across my forehead blown,
Or gazed upon the haloed brow
  Whose radiance lighted up my own.

And yet I stood in mute surprise
  Till all the vision passed away,
Nor once upraised my dazzled eyes,
  Nor oped my lips to whisper, "Stay!"

And slowly from my misty sight
  Did the sweet visitant depart, —
The angel-guest whose presence might
  Have re-illumed my darkened heart.

But ah, its memory haunts me yet, —
  And musing I can only say,
With starting tears of vain regret,
  "An angel passed me yesterday!"

THE CHEERFUL HEART.

Some deem the world a dreary place,
  Devoid of all redeeming merits,
But oh, it wears another face
  To cheerful and contented spirits!
Why ever dim joy's brightest rays,
  By gloomy fears of coming sorrows?
I always cheat the cloudy days
  With hopeful thoughts of happier morrows.

'T is true that "all things bright must fade" —
  That autumn's stern resistless powers,
With chilling wind and freezing shade
  Will blast the leaves and blight the flowers; —
For the departed summer's prime
  Let other hearts be vainly yearning,
But through the snows of winter time,
  I gladly watch for its returning.

'T is true life's sorrows every day
  Seem almost to outweigh its pleasures,
And death full often steals away
  The trusting heart's most cherished treasures; —

Let others mourn one dear one less,
And wildly weep o'er heart-strings riven,
I only joy that I possess
Another loving friend in heaven! —

'T is true the friends are sadly few
On whom we lean with trust unshaken,
And oft o'er those we fancied true,
Faith sighs to find herself mistaken.
I yield not to one vain regret,
When wayward fate hath so bereft me,
But only love more fondly yet
The dear ones still so kindly left me.

Though hope may cease to sing awhile,
And joy's sweet light seem slowly paling,
'T is better far to wear a smile,
For sighs and tears are unavailing.
Let other's weep that bright dreams fade,
And, weekly wearing sorrow's fetter,
Forever seek life's gloomiest shade, —
I love its cheering sunshine better! —

What though my lot of pain and toil
Be lowlier than my prouder brother's?
What though I heap no golden spoil,
The envy and the hate of others?

Let others seek the shining road,
  And walk with mammon's worldly minions,—
I joy that I've no wealth to load
  To earth my spirit's heavenward pinions!

Brightly may glisten glory's light,
  No envy in my bosom waking,
For Fame's proud wreath, though fair to sight,
  Oft blooms above a heart that's breaking.
The monarch's crown I covet not,
  And only pity those who wear it,
Desiring with my humble lot
  Only a cheerful heart to bear it!

NOVEMBER.

In the chill shadow of the songless wood,
  Of late so musical in the summer air,
Sits autumn, in her lonely solitude,
  Hiding her sad face with her nut-brown hair.

Crowned not with the bright garland she has worn
  In the sweet light of the October days,
For winter's hand the wreath has rudely torn,
  Blighted and faded, from its resting-place.

With angry haste he tears away its leaves,
  Crushing its flowers beneath his icy tread,
Then, half-repenting his unkindness, weaves
  A band of pearls around her drooping head.

Alas, the gift has chilled her to the heart; —
  And now with gentle touch and breathings low,
He lays the brown locks from her face apart,
  And wraps her in a winding-sheet of snow.

FLORENCE'S BIRTH-DAY.

"Florence, wake!" the birds are calling,
Brushing with their wings the dew,
But thé words which they are saying
None may know but me and you.
'T is your birth-day morning, dearest,
And the warbling songsters say,
"Baby Florence, darling Florence,
Two years old to-day!"

Ah, no father's lip may bless you, —
He is o'er the sea away;
Would his fond eyes might behold you,
Would he could be here to-day!
Could his loving arms enfold you,
Do you know what he would say?
"Baby Florence, darling Florence,
Two years old to-day!"

Never mother's heart clung closelier
  To her child than mine to you,
Gem of love's bright broken circle,
  Fresh and guileless, — pure and true!
Will life's thousand cares and changes
  Lure your heart from mine away?
Baby Florence, darling Florence,
    Two years old to-day!

Ah, my heart looks forward sadly
  To the path your feet must tread; —
Would it might be strown with roses,
  And their thorns be mine instead!
Happy one! no dark misgivings
  Make your merry heart less gay; —
Baby Florence, darling Florence,
    Two years old to-day!

And I will not dim the present,
  By foreboding future woe;
Grief and joy in life are mingled
  Wisely, since God wills it so,
And there is a watchful angel
  Who will hover round your way;
Baby Florence, darling Florence,
    Two years old to-day!

I will trust you with the Shepherd,
  Who, whene'er His young lambs faint,
Folds them softly in His bosom,
  Soothing every wailing plaint;
For I know His hand will lead you
  Safely through life's perilous way;
Baby Florence, darling Florence,
    Two years old to-day!

MARCH.

It is March, — the month of snow-drifts and of bleak and
boisterous weather,
When the winter bids defiance to the spring,
But on this delightful morning they walk smilingly together,
Lover-like, but with no lover's quarreling.

For the morn looks out in beauty, and the frost's enameled
painting
On the pane, is slowly melting in the sun, —
On the white hills in the distance, soft the foggy haze is
fainting,
From the eaves the drops are dripping, one by one.

Mossy knolls on yonder hill-side from the sinking snow
are peeping,
And the sunlight rests there lovingly and fair,
And an April breeze that wooingly from yonder wood is
sweeping,
Tells of young buds on the maple branches there.

I can close my eyes, and fancy as I feel upon my forehead
The fragrant wind, and hear its pleasant tune,
That it is a summer zephyr, and its balmy breath is borrowed
From the blossoming and budding of young June.

CLOVER BLOSSOMS.

I'VE read of roses till I tire of them,
  Of daffodils and myrtle-blossoms too, —
I'd rather have a fresh, sweet, home-like gem
  Like this I hold, unhackneyed, pure and new; —
My taste is rude; — I like not hot-house flowers, —
  Art, more than nature, breathes in their perfume;
They are unlike these children of the showers
  As carmine is unlike a natural bloom,
Poor exiles, city-born and city-bred,
  They tell no tales of nature's dewy bowers; —
Were I a bride, this morning to be wed,
  I'd slight those everlasting "orange-flowers,"
Of which, since Eve was bride, we've heard and read,
And loop the bridal veil with clover-blooms instead!

TO ONE DEPARTED.

IN the soft and pale spring sunlight,
In the summer's changing hues,—
In the ringing of the rain-drops,
In the dropping of the dews,
Comes a gentle spirit-whisper
Floating dreamily to me,
In its soft and soul-like accents,
Murmuring, lost one, of thee!

In the streamlet's gushing laughter,
In the night-wind's wailing moan,
In the breeze-rocked forest's music,
In the wild-bird's gladsome tone,
Still I hear that low sweet breathing
From the harp of memory,
On its viewless pinions bringing
Dearest one, a thought of thee!

In the wild-bee's drowsy humming,
'Mid the summer's flowering vines,
In the spirit-like complaining
Of the wind among the pines,—

In the thousand dreamy voices
  Of the earth and of the sea,
Cometh still that haunting whisper,
  Murmuring, lost one, of thee!

In the ocean's surging murmur,
  As its ceaseless song it weaves, —
In the light and playful rustle
  Of the wind among the leaves, —
Wheresoe'er my footsteps wander
  Cometh still that voice to me,
Like a sweet resounding echo,
  Murmuring ever, love, of thee!

TWO.

I AM the foot-stalk and she is the flower,—
I am the lattice and she is the vine;
My heart's a thirsty waste,—hers is the shower
Bringing refreshing and gladness to mine.

She is a sculptured dome,—I, the harsh granite;—
She is the virgin gold,—I, the rough ore;—
She is a perfect and beautiful plant,
I am the nebulous chaos of yore.

She is a living form; I am the marble
Which 'neath the chisel, may image her charms;—
My music breathes of art;—hers is the warble
Borne up to heaven, in the morning's blue calms.

Her mind, a polished gem, needs no attrition,
Mine is crude, shapeless, as won from the soil;
She, by a natural and easy transition,
Grows to the grace that I reach but by toil.

Mine is a power acquired, — hers was born with her, —
   Mine is a studied charm, — hers is her own;
She looks *down* on the world, — I look *up* thither, —
   I stand with thousands, but she stands alone.

I am the canvas whereon may be painted
   Shapes of strange beauty, — conceptions sublime, —
She a rare picture, — pure, beautiful, sainted,
   Sketched by the Master, to live for all time.

She is a spring; — I, the rock that stands by it;
   She is the calm bright sky, — I am the sea,
Mirroring softly its pure starry quiet; —
   This is the difference in my love and me!

TWENTY-ONE.

TWENTY-ONE! 't is yet youth's early morning,—
  Life's real, earnest strife is but begun,—
Yet there falls a stern mysterious warning
  O'er my soul, as clouds across the sun,
  And a voice says, "Work ere day be done!"

Twenty-one! and silently before me,
  Shade of the dead Past, I see thee rise;—
Cast not now thy mournful presence o'er me,
  Turn not on me thy reproachful eyes!
  Darkly on my heart their meaning lies.

For they ask me—"Hast thou raised one altar
  To the Spirit of the Good and True?
Wherefore do thy footsteps idly falter
  Thus at duty's gate, and pass not through,
  While theré yet remains so much to do?"

It is that my weak hands have no power,
  And I cannot labor as I would;
Lacking eloquence, and genius' dower,
  How can I achieve a single good?
  How be heard among the multitude?

Rouse thee, heart, from thine inactive slumber!
  Even the humblest has a sphere to fill,
And the deeds of every hour I number
  Help to swell the tide of good or ill; —
  Rouse! thy sloth may be atoned for still!

If I cause one heart to beat more lightly,
  If I soothe a grief or ease a pain,
If I make one tearful eye beam brightly,
  With the light of happiness again,
  I shall not have labored all in vain.

A DRY DITTY.

OH, there has been a weary time
Of heat and dust and blight,
Since rain has blest the earth, and fringed
The leaves with drops of light.
The river, shrunken in its bed,
Keeps sadly murmuring, —
The frogs are silent all the night,
They have no heart to sing!

Men make strange faces at the sky,
And "think it looks like rain" —
Ah, that their hopeful prophecies
Are ventured all in vain!
That "all signs fail in time of drought,"
They willingly allow,
And weather-wisdom everywhere
Is at a discount now!

On the parched roofs the shingles warp; —
The cisterns all are dry; —
The very spouts along the eaves
Yawn half-reproachfully;

And when to fan the passers-by,
  A cooling breeze is given,
Dust-clouds, like a remonstrance, rise
  Imploringly to heaven.

Ladies walk out, as, rain or shine,
  They always will and must,
But even their light foot-falls raise
  A choking whirl of dust.
Low slippers lose their witchery,
  White hose look sadly dim,
And little feet with gaiter-boots
  Are in a sorry trim.

Come to the thirsty earth, oh, rain!
  Come to the yellow grass!
Come to the crispéd leaves, that curl,
  Dry rustling, as I pass!
Come, that all green things may rejoice!
  Come, that the patient boat
Moored where the river used to be,
  May be once more afloat!

Come that the school-boys, who erewhile
  Mope listless through the street,
May wade along in road-side ponds,
  And wash their dusty feet!

Let mothers scold o'er muddy clothes,
  And warning threats repeat,
Boys never can be boys but once,
  And rain is such a treat!

Come rain, dear rain! 'mid nature's friends
  I prize thee most of all;—
Alas, that one who loves thee so
  Could glory in thy fall!—
Joy!—one of larger faith than I,
  Most trustingly maintains
That "*that after such a drought as this,*
  It almost always rains!"

THE BENT OF THE TWIG.

THE moon is out in beauty, silvering
Hill, field and forest with her icy light,
And as I gaze, a tiny, toddling thing,
With pattering feet, and face upraised and bright,
Comes to my side; — I raise her in my arms
Placing her feet upon the window-sill,
And long she gazes on the landscape's charms,
Laughing as all delighted babies will:
Grasps at the stars, which far in dizzy space,
Lie thick as blossoms in the lap of June, —
Then with lips parted, and uplifted face,
Raises her arms and tries to kiss the moon.
"*How soon*," says one whose face I just discover,
"*That child, like all her sex, aspires to things above her!*"

THE WHITE DOVE.

Over the misty mountains,
Over the sounding sea,
Far through the dreamy distance
Came a white dove to me.

Sorrow upon my harp-strings
Lay like corroding rust,
Darkly hope's holy radiance
Faded, an empty trust, —
Till my o'erburdened spirit,
Wildered by doubts and fears,
Saw only clouds and darkness
Dimly, through falling tears, —

When over the misty mountains,
Over the surging sea,
Far through the dreamy distance,
Came a white dove to me.

Spoke I in trembling whispers
Thus to the spirit-bird: —
"Who in the land of shadows,
Who hath my plaining heard?
Art thou some friend departed,
Come to my heart again?"
And a sweet voice rose clearly,
Soft as the summer rain: —

"Over the misty mountains,
Over the sounding sea,
Far through the dreamy distance,
Lone one, I come to thee!

"I am no friend departed
Over life's mystic main,
Coming in clouds and darkness
Back to thy heart again; —
I am the might, the power,
Conqueror all above,
I am the joy, the sunshine
Lighting earth's darkness, — Love!

"And over the misty mountains,
Over the surging sea,
Far through the dreamy distance,
Lone one, I come to thee!"

Then the white dove which never,
Never will more depart,
Folded its snowy pinions
Over my gladdened heart;
Thrillingly sweet and gentle
Is the low song it sings —
"Rest thee, thou weary spirit,
Under my shielding wings!"

Over the misty mountains,
Over the sounding sea,
Far through the dreamy distance
Came a white dove to me!

A LULLABY.

Come to my bosom, my only, my own,
Thou from whose forehead heaven's light hath not flown, —
Time hath not yet, with his pinions of gloom,
Scattered thy young heart's first beautiful bloom, —
Thou art unchilled by the shadows of years,
Thou hast not gathered life's harvest of tears ; —
Fondly I clasp thee, beloved, in my arms, —
Freshness and purity, — these are thy charms!

Roses are sweetest when partly blown,
Love is most blessed when scarcely known,
Life is brightest when just begun,
And thus are all dear things, belovèd one!
But my heart, as thy tiny form I press,
Whispers — "I never can love thee less!"

When summer's fierce heats in the sultry air quiver,
T is cheering to list to the cool sound of a river,
And thus to my heart comes the voice of thy laughter,
With its fresh rippling gush,, and its sweet echo after.

'My love, like a vine, clasps its tendrils about thee,
And desolate, lone, were my being without thee;
Oh, we'll walk hand in hand through life's changeable
weather,
And when death's summons comes, we'll obey it together!

Morning is brightest when it is breaking,
Music is sweetest just at its waking,
Stars are most beautiful when first they glimmer,
Time renders all bright things colder and dimmer;
God keep thy heart, through life's trials estranging,
Constant and spotless,—unchanged and unchanging!

Weary of life's dull monotonous hum,
Till my tired heart sinks, all voiceless and dumb,
Weary of following one dreary way
Aimless and passionless, day after day,
Gladly to greet thee my worn spirit flies,
Light of my loneliness, — star of my skies!
Fondly I clasp thee again in my arms, —
Freshness and purity — these are thy charms!

Roses are sweetest when partly blown,
Love is most blessed when scarcely known,
Life is brightest when just begun,
And thou art now loveliest, dearest one!
But my fond heart breathes, as I kiss thy brow,
"I never can love thee less than now!"

THY BLESSING.

I CANNOT come to thee as in the days
Long past, but not forgotten; — I have been
Since then through many dark and dreary ways,
Through much of care, and weariness, and sin.

Thy path lies calmly 'mid the pastures green
And the still waters of the better land,
While vainly yearning for that rest serene,
My feet still press life's burning desert-sand.

And yet, in spirit and in truth I come
To crave thy blessing, ere I wander far
Across the waste of ocean's plashing foam,
Obedient to my chosen guiding-star.

And by a gentle faith, which long hath shed
Its radiance on a pathway dim and cold,
I feel thy shadowy hand upon my head,
And hear thy whispered blessing as of old.

My glad heart rises every fear above,
  Strengthened by the inspiring words to say, —
"I will be true to duty and to love,
  And follow wheresoe'er they lead the way!"

THE SUNKEN ROCK.

SHE launched her boat at break of day,
And o'er the waters sailed away.
"Oh pray," she said, "no billow dark
May whelm me and my little bark!"

"Oh may no tempest's raging wrath
Sweep wildly o'er my watery path,
No cloud the clear sky darken o'er,
Until I reach the other shore!"

The sea was smooth, the sky was fair,
And softly breathed the wafting air,
And leaning o'er the vessel's side,
The maiden watched the waves divide.

And heard the soft contiuous note
Sung by the waters round her boat,
While flakes of foam, like lilies, lay
Whitely along the rippling way.

Then sung the maiden joyfully,
"There's not a cloud to dim the sky,
How pleasantly, the bright waves o'er,
I hasten to the other shore!"

When lo! with rude and stunning shock,
The frail keel struck a sunken rock,
And though no cloud the calm sky crossed,
The maiden and the boat were lost!

And as the fated bark went down,
A voice the waters could not drown,
Said — "Fear thou not the tempest's shock,
But oh, beware the sunken rock!"

THE UNBIDDEN GUEST.

Mirth and music are here to-night,
  Red lips murmur and bright eyes glance,
Forms of beauty with motion light
  Float and whirl in the dizzy dance.

Up and down in a living stream
  Winds the waltz like a wreath of flowers,
Rich robes rustle and white arms gleam,
  Light feet fall like the beat of showers.

Yonder, there where the shadow lies,
  Pale and earnest a face appears,
Gazing at me with steady eyes,
  Eyes whose brightness is that of tears.

See ye, gay ones, the pale sad face,
  Gazing forth from the shadow there?
Can it be that the form I trace
  Is no other than empty air?

Lightly, brightly, the dance whirls by,
Pausing not where the shadow lies
Dim and silent, — and only I
See the face with the haunting eyes.

Sweet the calm on the brow that lies,
Sweet the smile on the silent lips,
Still and deep are the shadowy eyes,
Like a lake where the lily dips.

"Guest unbidden, why haunt me so?
All the day are my thoughts of thee,
All the night does thy memory flow
Over my soul like a whelming sea!

"Ever into my dim lone room
Comest thou nightly, with even's star, —
Why dost thou come where light and bloom,
Beauty and love and gladness are?"

Clasping closely my passive hands,
Comes the presence and walks with me, —
In and out with the joyous bands
Pass together the bond and free.

And as we wander to and fro
Under the lamp-light's searching shine,
Little the eyes which see me, know
Spirit fingers are clasping mine!

TWENTY-TWO.

SMILINGLY day's wearied monarch
  Lays aside her golden crown,
And o'er earth's calm breast, the twilight
  Shakes her shadowy tresses down.
With white forehead pure and saintly
  Comes the moon of memories,
And upon the dim earth faintly
  Look the loving Pleiades.

Little one, with face uplifted
  Softly to the failing light,
And thy soft hair brightly drifted
  Backward from thy forehead white, —
Come, while yet yon lonely wild-bird
  Warbles forth his farewell trills,
And the hem of day's bright garment
  Lies along the western hills, —

Come and see how fast the summer
  Flees before October's tread,
With her garments rent and faded,
  And her garlands sere and dead.
Bright the frozen dew-drops glitter
  Lying on her soft brown hair,
And her sighing, sad and bitter,
  Burdens all the golden air.

Two-and-twenty years this even
  Since a mother's yearning prayer
Blest a young child, newly given
  To the world's unloving care;
Two-and-twenty years this even!
  Just as now the stars looked down, —
Just as now, night's calm-browed empress
  Wore her pearl and silver crown; —

Yet all else is strangely altered;
  Ah, for many lonesome years,
O'er that mother's lowly grave-mound
  Have the violets dropped their tears;
Weeping not that she so early
  In life's battle sunk and died,
But that one she blessed in dying,
  Is not sleeping by her side!

Little one, with face uplifted
  Softly in the silver light,
And thy bright hair backward drifted —
  Know'st thou 't is my birth-day night?
Know'st thou, as we kneel together
  Where the moonlight floods the floor,
On my conscious head in blessing.
  Rests that mother's hand once more?

MAGIC MIRRORS.

A FAIR young child with heart of glee
Stands prattling by its mother's knee,
And as her eyes reflect the smile
Brightening her darling's face the while,
"Oh, mother, dear," the cherub cries,
"I see a baby in your eyes!"

The mother stoops and playfully
Raising the infant to her knee,
Gazes within the azure deeps
Where joy's bright meaning never sleeps;—
A pale sad *woman* she descries,
Out-gazing from her baby's eyes!

"Ah, eyes tell truth," she sighs at last,—
"Yours speak your *future*,—mine my *past;*
For in your radiant orbs I see
A prophecy of days to be,
And in my own dimmed eyes, appears
A glimpse of childhood's vanished years!"

THE HAUNTED RIVER.

I SIT by a beautiful river,
  Whose waves, dancing on to the sea,
Are kissing each other in gladness,
  And laughing like children in glee.

It flows amid flower-gemmed meadows,
  And eddies through blossomy dells,
And, to every fresh leaf-spray that greets it,
  A tale of new melody tells.

When twilight with covetous fingers
  Afar in the shadowy west,
Has gathered the roses of sunset,
  And hidden them under her vest, —

I love by its margin to wander,
  For sweetest of music to me
Is the song rippling up from its bosom,
  In numbers triumphant and free.

The charm of an olden tradition
   Hangs over the beautiful place,
Investing its wildering sweetness
   With a sacred and mystical grace.

'T is a tale of a sunny-eyed maiden
   Who dwelt by the murmuring stream,
With a form and a face which were fairer
   Than the shapes in a summer-night's dream.

But there came a dark sorrow, that blighted
   Her heart to its innermost core,
And the gladness returned to her spirit,
   And the smile to her sweet lips no more.

One night in the beautiful season
   Which follows the summer's decline,
When beams from the fair face of heaven
   A smile that is almost divine, —

When her chaplet of crimson and golden
   The goddess of autumn-time weaves,
And berries like clusters of rubies
   Hide under the emerald leaves, —

She parted the curls from her forehead,
   And bound them with glittering gems,
And looped up their rich glossy masses
   With lilies and daffodil stems, —

And decked in pure snowy-white garments
  Befitting a newly-made bride,
She loosened her boat from its mooring,
  And rowed o'er the glistening tide.

And when the glad morning was shaking
  The light from her tresses of gold,
And the folds of her many-hued mantle
  Again in the east were enrolled,

And the wood-birds, to welcome her coming
  Were warbling their merriest strain,
The boat lay alone on the water
  But the maiden returned not again.

And 't is said in the gathering twilight
  Of autumn's soft whispering eves,
When sweetly the river is singing
  Its song to the listening leaves,

When the wind, with a mother's devotion
  Has rocked the faint blossoms to rest,
And the white moonlight lies like a spirit
  Asleep on the river's soft breast,

With a dipping of shadowy paddles
  Which noiselessly tremble and gleam,
A boat, like a silvery crescent
  Comes floating adown the bright stream.

And there, with her lily-twined tresses,
  A snowy-white bridal array,
The beautiful maiden sits guiding
  The boat on its star-lighted way.

Ah! oft have I mused on the story,
  Alone in this shadowy place,
Till I almost could see in the waters
  The gleam of a beautiful face, —

Till dimly my watching eyes pictured
  In a far away curve of the stream,
The spirit-like boat of the maiden
  And her white garments' quivering gleam.

CHARMED.

TURN away thy strange soft eyes,
They oppress me with their beauty,
And the light that in them lies
Lures me far from right and duty.

I have watched their dazzling beam
Till my very life and being,
Thought and speech and motion seem
Centered in the sense of seeing.

Though the fire of thy strange eyes
To my very heart is burning,
Still my wildered spirit sighs
Deeply for their soft returning.

For my all of bliss in life
I have known since first I met thee, —
Ah! it is a weary strife
This vain struggle to forget thee!

WHERE CHARLIE DIED.

THERE seems a sacred presence here,
  A gloom as of approaching night,
For one whose smile to us was dear
  Here bowed to death's remorseless blight.
The youngest of our household band,
  Fair-browed, and gay, and sunny-eyed,
Unclasped from ours his little hand
  And in his childish beauty died.

They said he died; — it seems to me
  That, after hours of pain and strife,
He slept, one even, peacefully,
  And woke toeverlasting life;
And mirth's glad voice, and laughter's cheer
  May ring through all the house beside,
But quiet sadness reigneth here,
  Since darling baby Charlie died.

Oh! when my heart, oppressed by care,
  Grows faint to find its heaven unwon,
And shrinks from life's vain hollow glare
  As flowers beneath the August sun, —
I love to seek this shadowy room,
  By memory sadly sanctified,
And linger in the eloquent gloom
  Which hallows it since Charlie died.

And ever as I enter here,
  With noiseless steps and low-drawn breath,
There seems an unseen presence near,
  For here the twilight gate of death
Once, on a holy summer night,
  By angel hands was swung aside,
Opening from darkness into light
  When darling baby Charlie died.

THE MINSTREL.

One there was, though fair and young,
  Blest with song's most wondrous dower,
And a skilful hand she flung
  O'er a lyre of magic power.
Beauty fashioned not her face
  In a mould of faultless seeming,
But it wore thought's earnest trace,
  And the light of soul, bright beaming.

In her eyes so strangely bright,
  Full of deep and dewy splendor,
When their soft and changeful light
  Told of feeling true and tender, —
In her haughty brow of snow,
  In the tear her cheek impearling, —
In the sweet voice trembling low,
  In her soft lip proudly curling;
In her song's melodious art,
  Sweetness from its grief deriving,
One might read that in her heart
  Pride and wretchedness were striving:

Though the worldly thoughtless throng
  Paused awhile to list in wonder
The proud triumph of her song,
  And the anguish wailing under.
When she sung of brows of snow,
  No one knew that hers was aching,
When of hearts in joy's bright glow,
  No one cared that hers was breaking; —
When she sung of smiling eyes,
  No one saw that hers were tearful.
And her young life's closest ties
  Rent by anguish strong and fearful.
Loneliness weighed down her heart, —
  Love or friendship never found her, —
Not one soul with hers had part,
  'Mid the thousands gathered round her;
For the great world looked on her
  As on one too highly gifted
For a mortal love to stir, —
  And no pleading voice was lifted.

Thus she sang, day after day,
  No one heeding, no one caring,
Till her heart, once light and gay,
  Grew dark, heavy and despairing, —
Till her song of dreamings bright
  Changed to murmurs sad and bitter,
And her soft eyes' loving light
  Grew a cold and icy glitter;

Till her eyelids drooped in sleep,
  And her song was hushed forever,
And she sunk in slumber deep,
  Tired of life's long vain endeavor;—
And her last brief trembling breath
  Fell upon the deaf air only,—
Who shall answer for her death
  Thus uncared-for, sad and lonely?

Every feeling unreturned,
  Each affection unrequited,
Every prayer for love that's spurned,
  Every lofty hope that's blighted,
Is a deep and bitter wrong
  In the eyes of the All-seeing,
And amid life's varied throng,
  Many a heart deplores their being.

Who shall answer for the grief
  In the minstrel's being centered?
On what cold heart's darkened leaf
  Shall the heavy sin be entered?

DANDELIONS.

Oh, dandelions, ye are here again
  With June's glad sunshine in your golden eyes!
Far as the eye may reach, o'er hill and plain,
  A yellow smile on nature's fair face lies.
Oh, bright-eyed ones! ye are the only flowers
  Which come to me as ye in childhood came;
All things seem changed to me, since those bright hours,—
  All but your faces,—they are just the same,—
And I retrace my path of toil and care
  Back to the realm of toys and skipping-ropes,
And blow your gossamer seed-globes high in air,
  And watch their rise,—as rose my early hopes!
Too truly said,—for like your feathery crown
I've found those hopes, since then, most literally *down!*

THE HAND IN MINE.

A HAND like the leaf of a blush-rose,
O'er which the bright dew-pearls are strown,
Forever through sunlight and shadow
Is lovingly clasped in my own.

If I roam through the summer-time forests,
Or climb the steep slope of the hills, —
Or rest in the blossomy shadows
Which curtain the course of the rills, —

If I search for the first timid flowers
The spring's budding mosses among,
Or sit in the shine of the fire-light
When the evenings are wintry and long, —

If I stray where the world's striving voices
Are sounding, contentious and loud,
Or seek in my own quiet chamber,
Relief from the turbulent crowd, —

In the bright hours which follow the dawning,
  Or in the broad daylight of noon,
Or when the blithe cricket is singing
  At eve his monotonous tune, —

Or when the thick tresses of midnight
  On earth's silent bosom are thrown,
The hand with its soft, clasping fingers
  Lies lovingly still in my own.

And when the pale messenger cometh,
  Whose smile hath a promise divine,
Will they lay me away from my idol,
  And take the dear fingers from mine?

Oh, no! let us yield up together
  The last brief and quivering breath,
And the hands which in life never parted,
  Be still undivided in death!

AGAIN.

Mother, I come to thee again,
  As in my shadowed hours of old,
But oh, I find thee not as then,—
  The sod above thy heart is cold;
I hear no more thy whisper's thrill,
  I feel no more thy lip's soft touch,—
Thy voice is mute, thy heart is still,
  And I am changed almost as much!

For fate my trembling steps has led
  Where sorrow's bitter waters swell,
And showers from love's pure fountain shed,
  Have changed to tear-drops as they fell;
And now for many a weary year,
  Since I have strayed away from thee,
Thy low neglected pillow here
  Has only seemed like home to me.

And though across my forehead now,
  Time's lines and furrows are not drawn,
Though years rest lightly on my brow,
  The spring-time of my heart is gone;—
And I could envy thy sweet rest,
  Thy calm release from pain and care,—
Could gladly sleep upon thy breast,
  And find a blessed solace there!

MY WORLD.

I HAVE a world, a radiant world,
In which I dwell alone,
Where earthly cares and woes and fears,
Are never felt or known;
No foot unwelcome enters there,—
I hold the mystic key;
Its golden portals, wide and fair,
Ope never but for me.

There are no sorrows in my world,
No anguish and no tears;
Its beauty and its happiness
Fade not with fading years;
There are no tempests in its sky,
No clouds by lightning riven;
No gloom or darkness ever falls
Athwart its summer-heaven.

No southern clime has flowers so sweet,
With hues so rich and bright,
As those which blossom in my world,
Unchilled by winter's blight:
Amid its gardens broad and fair
No stricken blossom grieves, —
My world has autumn's gorgeous dyes,
But not its withered leaves.

And there are princely palaces,
And towers high and fair,
Rearing their snowy battlements
Against the purple air;
And stately domes and marble founts,
And castles proud and grand,
Are there, beneath the rosy skies
Of my enchanted land.

And there are birds whose colored wings
Fan fragrance from the bowers,
As in and out, in sun and shade,
They float like wingéd flowers;
And when upon their shining plumes,
I watch the rainbow gleams,
I hear such songs as other ears
Hear only in their dreams.

No frowning storm-cloud broods in wrath
  My pleasant world above,
For all the air is music there,
  And every thought is love;
"The wind is never in the east"—
  But zephyrs bland and sweet
Blow soft, and shake the blossoms down
  In showers at my feet.

You think my world a lifeless realm,
  A fair dead solitude,
Where loneliness and mystery
  And voiceless silence brood;
But it has shapes of radiant grace,
  With faces sweet and fair,
With brows unmarked by toil and grief,
  And eyes undimmed by care.

These be the angel ministers
  Who shield me with their wings,
And sing me sweet unearthly songs
  Of high and holy things;
Who fill my heart with happiness
  Which nothing can destroy,
And make my life, despite its clouds,
  A blessing and a joy.

And when, like sad foreboding clouds,
  Heavy with autumn rain,
The shadows of this outer life
  Fall dark on heart and brain,
I have a refuge from their wrath
  Which others may not see,
For into my ideal world
  They cannot follow me.

RESIGNATION.

THERE is no sister-band, however tended,
But one young bride is there ;—
There is no fire-side, howsoe'er defended,
But has one vacant chair.

Our home is full of mingled smiles and sighing,
Our fairest one has fled!
And baby Ned, for his lost sister crying,
Will not be comforted!

Let us be patient! these severe afflictions
Not from the ground arise,
But oftentimes, celestial benedictions
Assume hymeneal guise.

We see but dimly through the mists and vapors,
But, drying sorrow's damps,
We read her marriage notice in the papers,
And trim hope's brightest lamps.

Marriage is nought; — what seems so is transition;
    The life she lived of late
Is but a suburb to the life elysian
    Yclept the wedded state.

She is not dead, — the child of our affection,
    But gone unto that school,
Wherein she lays aside our fond protection
    To own a husband's rule.

In that great cloister's stillness and seclusion,
    By his old mother led,
Safe from "young company" and mirth's intrusion,
    She lives, — the same as dead.

Day after day we think what she is doing
    In those old dismal rooms,
Year after year, her toilsome way pursuing
    With stew-pans, mops and brooms.

Sometime will visit her, to keep unbroken
    The bond which nature gives,
Thinking that our kind pity, though unspoken,
    May cheer her where she lives.

Not as a girl shall we again behold her,
    For when, with rapture wild,
In our embraces we again enfold her,
    She will not be a child, —

But a staid matron, in her husband's mansion,
Clothed with a graver grace,
And beautiful with womanhood's expansion,
Shall we behold her face.

And though we see, with anger and emotion,
How poorly she is dressed,
In a cheap gingham, which with fond devotion,
She dignifies her "best,"

We will be patient, and assuage the feeling,
The little time we stay,
Our pity and our sympathy concealing
Until we come away!

BETTER THAN BEAUTY.

Ye may praise the charms of a beautiful face,
And dream of a fairy form,
For me, I care not for outward grace,
If the heart be true and warm;
The witching glances which beauty throws,
Enchantingly bright may be,
But the eye where love's warm sunshine glows,
Is dearer by far to me!

Ye may tell of lips like the coral's hue
Or rose-buds wet with showers,
But a lip whose breathings are fond and true,
Be mine, in my sadder hours,—
For when by sorrow too deeply stirred
My lonely heart may be,
From loving lips one gentle word
Is happiness to me!

Ye may tell of hands which are small and slight,
All daintily smooth and fair,
Whose taper fingers are soft and white
As the lily's petals are,
But a hand that will answer my own close clasp
Fondly and fervently,
With a cordial warmth in its friendly grasp,
Is dearer by far to me!

Ah, beauty has magical charms, if seen
In lip, or brow, or eye,
But a sweeter beauty than this, I ween,
In the hidden heart may lie; —
And lovely a face with beauty's glow
To other eyes may be,
But a beautiful face with no heart below
Seems mockery to me!

SEVENTEEN.

Seventeen long years ago! and still
  The hillock newly-heaped I see,
Which hid beneath its heavy chill
  One who has never died to me; —
And since, the leaves which o'er it wave
  Have been kept green by raining tears;
Strange how the shadow of a grave
  Could fall across so many years!

Seventeen long years ago! No cross,
  No urn nor monument is there,
But drooping leaves and starry moss
  Bend softly in the summer air;
The one I would have died to save
  Sleeps sweetly, free from griefs and fears;
Strange how the shadow of a grave
  Could fall across so many years!

Seventeen long years ago! I see
  The hand I held so long in vain,
The lips I pressed despairingly
  Because they answered not again:
I see again the shining wave
  Of the dark hair be-gemmed with tears,—
Strange how the shadow of a grave
  Could fall across so many years!

Seventeen long years ago! The hand
  Then fondly clasped, still holds my own,
Leading me gently to the land
  Where storm and shadow are unknown;
The summons which I gladly crave
  Will come like music to my ears,
And the chill shadow of the grave
  Be changed to light, ere many years!

"THE GOOD TIME COMING."

I SAW her on the sidewalk yesterday,
Tripping along with brisk and airy tread
Over the new-fallen snow, which thinly lay
Along her path; — she raised her pretty head,
Bringing to view a very lovely face,
And casting a coquettish glance around,
She set her foot upon a treacherous place
And down she went, astonished to the ground!
Down, — yet no sooner down than up again
With an elastic spring the fair one came, —
And such a rosy rising! I maintain
I've seen Aurora wrap the east in flame
With blush less burning; — but with glad surprise
I joyed that *woman had, at last, a "chance to rise!"*

ALLIE.

'T is a bleak November night,
  Fraught with storm and cloud and glow,
But the fire burns warm and bright
  In my cosy little room;
I am sitting here alone,
  And the patter of the rain,
And the wind's complaining sound
  Wake strange echoes in my brain;
Oh, if you were only here,
                Allie, dear!

Shadows quiver to and fro
  On the wall in seeming glee,
And ripe, red-cheeked apples glow
  In the firelight temptingly;
Just across the heart-rug there
  Is a most inviting seat,—
An old-fashioned easy-chair
  And a cushion for your feet;
Oh, if you were only here,
                Allie, dear!

I can almost see you now
  Sitting in that easy-chair
With a smile upon your brow
  Such as only you can wear;
With your large, shy loving eyes
  Saddened by no thought of care,
While the golden firelight lies
  Crown-like on your shining hair; —
Ah, methinks you must be here,
          Allie, dear!

But the vision fades away; —
  I am sitting here alone, —
And the firelight's fading ray
  Shines a moment and is gone.
Vacant stands the easy-chair,
  Fled is the illusion sweet,
But upon the window there
  Still the beating rain-drops beat,
And I still wish you were here,
          Allie, dear!

ONE NIGHT.

Daylight had waned, slowly and gloomily,
Dying as though unwilling to depart,
And heavier clouds than draped the frowning sky,
Hung darkly round my heart.

For the sweet angel-presence, kindly given
By the Good Father, — like a thought of Him,
To form one link between my heart and heaven,
Was growing faint and dim.

She was my all; — her hand the only stay
That held me to the earth; — in agony
I felt its grasp grow weaker, day by day, —
How could I see her die?

I laid the white face from my lips away,
And folded the pale hands away from mine,
And with a choking effort, strove to say
"Lord, not *my* will, but *Thine!*"

But duty bowed to love, that dark hour;
  My torn heart, shrinking from the bitter cup,
Closed round its idol with a passionate power,
  And would not yield it up.

When suddenly methought the veil was riven
  That hides the mystic future from our eyes,
And strangely to my wondering gaze were given
  Its mighty mysteries.

I saw a wanderer with weary tread
  Toiling along life's rough uneven way,
Whence cares and griefs, like shadows dark and dread,
  Obscured each cheering ray.

Long years of time and trial had laid waste
  The fresh pure charms which youth had gloried in,
And on the lip and cheek and brow were traced
  Sorrow and care and sin.

Along the rugged pathway, hard and steep,
  The pilgrim wandered, in the darkness wild.
And as she turned her face aside to weep,
  I knew it was *my child!*

The vision passed; — and I was bending still
  Beside the pillow of the suffering one;
The little hand in mine was yet more chill,
  The breathing almost done.

Calm, — almost thankful, — without word or sigh,
From the white brow I wiped the gathering dews,
When like a harp-note floating from on high
Came the low whisper — "Choose!"

Then from my breast I laid the drooping head,
And folded the pale hands away from mine,
And calmly, without tear or struggle, said,
"Lord, not *my* will, but *Thine!*"

"TRUE LOVE CAN NE'ER FORGET."

Oh, say not love made your pathway pleasant
With blessèd radiance in days gone by,—
The love that is past was never present,
For *true* love's brightness can never die!

I have no faith in transient passion.
How true soever it seem to be,
Which, like a bonnet, goes out of fashion,
As soon as it loses its novelty.

I know there are,—and their name is legion,—
Who look through vapors and darkness far,
To where in its own pure cloudless region,
Is the holy shining of love's sweet star;

And eager to clasp the coveted glory,
They wander wide in a fruitless quest,
And like the spirit in Bible story,
Walk through dry places, and find no rest;

Till seeing a fire-fly's fickle glancing,
They follow its fitful brightness far, —
'T is gained, — and they cry with joy entrancing,
"Eureka! see, I have found the star!"

Its light is feeble and faint and dying —
Grows daily dimmer and fades at last,
And then they say, with a transient sighing,
"Once, love was mine, — but the charm is past!"

But not by the loss is life o'erclouded, —
The heart is light as before it came,
Or, if a moment by sorrow shrouded,
Soon re-illumed by another flame.

Oh, fools and blind! that an insect's shining
Can lure your eyes from the star above!
That ye follow and clasp it, ne'er divining
Its radiance is not the light of love!

While love, *true* love, from its holy station,
Not changeful, though mortals deem it so,
Looks down with a smile of sweet compassion,
On the poor mistaken souls below!

Then say not love made your pathway pleasant
With transient radiance, in days gone by,
The love that is past was never present,
For *true* love's brightness can never die!

Let trust no more to the cheat be given,
But lift your eyes through the darkness far
To where, from its own unclouded heaven,
Floats down the glory of love's pure star!

TO MY NAMESAKE.

And have they called thee by my name, sweet child?
To me it had no sound of harmony
Till since thou hast beneath its burden smiled, —
Has it not caught new melody from thee?
Some names bring blessings with them; — if this be
Of those, a double share of joys is thine,
For it has wasted none of them on *me*; —
Thy young pure heart deserves them more than mine.
I had despaired of greatness, — my interests
Aspired not to the lofty or sublime,
And dreamed not of renown, — but when, years hence,
As faith declares will be revealed by time,
Thou to the laurel-crown hast proved thy claim,
My name.—for it is *thine*,—will grace "the scroll of Fame!"

TO A SINGER.

Daughter of melody!
The clear soft notes of thy soaring strain
Fall back on my listening heart again
As the first bright drops of the silver rain
On the breast of the quiet sea!

Child of the seraph strain!
Thou who sweepest my full heart's strings,
Thou who unbindest my spirit's wings,
Scattering the sorrow that round them clings,
Sing to me once again!

Daughter of music, come!
Come once more with thy witching song
Trembling my rapt soul's chords along,
Till care is forgotten, and grief, and wrong,
Make in my heart thy home!

Come, and enraptured long
From the first faint gleam of the morning bright,
Till I lose thine eyes' bewildering light
In the gathering shades of approaching night,
I'll listen thy magic song.

Thou wert not formed for earth, —
Thou seemest a spirit, who sits and sings
With eyes uplifted and folded wings, —
And pure heart dreaming of holy things, —
Thou art of heavenly birth!

TO ONE OF LITTLE FAITH.

Doubt me not, oh, timid heart,
Though our paths lie far apart,
And though long our parting be,
If you love me, trust in me!

My deep love, undimmed, can bear
Time and distance, grief and care,
But distrust its death would be, —
If you love me, trust in me!

Doubt me not, beloved! though far
Vast and wide beween us are
Miles of prairie, leagues of sea,
If you love me, trust in me!

Though long years may leave their trace,
Ere we meet, on heart and face,
Dare not doubt my constancy, —
If you love me, trust in me!

Tempt me not to think your heart
Has of love's high faith no part, —
This the proving test shall be,
If you love me, trust in me!

TWICE-TOLD.

THERE is something I would tell you
  If it would not make you frown,
If it would not bring so closely
  Round your face those tresses brown,
If it would not make your lashes
  Droop so beautifully down!

There is something I would ask you
  If I thought you'd answer "Yes,"—
If you would not coldly scatter
  All my daring dreams of bliss,
If you'd crown with sweet approval
  All my hopes of happiness!

May I whisper? What I'd tell you
  Is,—*I love you,—you alone,*—
What I'd ask you is,—*oh, dearest
  Will you,—will you be mine own?*
Nay, look up,—I've only told you
  Something which you long have known!

A PORTRAIT.

SHE is all angles, — and her thin hair stays
Tortured in many a quaint elaborate crook, —
Just where 't is placed; and in the hottest days
Her sharp face has a pinched, half-frozen look;
The "milk of human kindness" in her heart
Soured before the cream rose; — probably
'T was the reflection of her face, in part,
Which caused the metamorphosis, — ah, me,
Tartaric acid never was so tart
As heart and face combined are wont to be!
Her voice is audible vinegar, boiled down,
And oh, if *that's* a smile, heaven save me from her frown!

MY WIFE AND CHILD.

I DREAM; — my gentle wife is near, —
  A girlish figure, small and slight;
Say, shall I sketch her picture, ere
  She passes out of sight?
Hers is no beauty strange and rare,
  Fashioned by rapturous poet's rule;
All hearts might deem her very fair,
  And not one, beautiful.
Not beautiful to painters' eyes,
Because her noblest beauty lies
Not in her features' faultless grace,
But the sweet *meaning* of her face.

A look of patient gentleness
  On lip and brow serenely lies;
And oh, a world of tenderness
  Shines softly in her sunny eyes!
Her lips — to me no "rose-buds wet"
  One half so beautiful could be,

I love them that they never yet
  Spoke one unloving word to me.
There is a sweet and nameless grace
Floating around her form and face, —
The beauty of a lofty soul
Illumes and beautifies the whole.

And when the tiresome day is gone
And the sweet evening time comes on,
And wearied out with toil and care,
I sink into my study-chair, —
Closing my eyes to curtain out
The vexing shapes of fear and doubt, —
A tiny foot, with noiseless glide
Comes stealing softly to my side —
Bright curls adown my shoulders twine,
And little fingers hide in mine ; —
Oh, I can meet, with dauntless heart,
  The sternest, darkest ills of life,
With such a guardian as *thou* art
  My own belovèd wife !

My child ! my darling bright-eyed boy !
  A happy, laughter-loving sprite,
Whose heart is mirth, whose life is joy,
  Undimmed by shade or blight.
He has his mother's curls of gold,
  His laugh has just her ringing tone,

And in his features I behold
  The softened likeness of my own.
And gazing, oft I wander back
Along my boyhood's flowery track, —
I roam again beside the stream,
I see again the pebbles gleam,
And stooping, see, or seem to see
My face reflected back to me!

My wife and child! my all on earth!
  Oh, what were life, bereft of them?
Beside their love, how little worth
  Seems glory's brightest diadem!
My wife and child! — these are the charms
  Which makes me cling to earth, — I rise
To circle them in love's fond arms,
  And in the act, — unclose my eyes.

Where, where am I? and where are *they?*
Alas, the dream has passed away!
I sit here in my darkening room,
Alone amid the dusky gloom, —
Ay, all alone, — no wife, no child, —
A day-dream hath my heart beguiled; —
Alas, that airy fancy's sway
  Should play this roguish trick with me!
My wife and child, I sigh to say,
  Are yet — alas! — *are yet to be!*

RE-UNITED.

WHERE upon a silent shore
Sobbing surges evermore
Beat and break in blinding tears,
Watched I, with despairing fears;

Seeing two, in youth's bright glow
Wandering wearily and slow,
Clasping closely hand in hand,
O'er the waste of yielding sand.

One a proud and noble youth
With a heart of love and truth,
And with early manhood's grace
Mantling o'er his form and face;

One a young and timid bride
Clinging fondly to his side,
With the orange-blossoms fair
Yet unwithered in her hair.

Young and hopeful, loved and fair,
Why so sadly walked they there,
Thus with brief uneven breath
By the surging sea of death?

Solemnly and silently
Passed they toward the heaving sea,
And at last with weary feet,
Stood where beach and billow meet.

From the shadow evermore
Shrouding all the other shore,
Slowly, without oar or sail
Came a boatman, chill and pale.

Softly came the boat to land
Where upon the crumbling sand,
Waiting calmly, side by side
Stood the bridegroom and his bride.

Then with pale but smiling face,
Gently from its soft embrace
He unwound her clasping arm,
And his voice was clear and calm:

"Fare thee well, beloved! I go
With the boatman, pale as snow;
Fare thee well! — beyond the tide
Will I wait for thee, my bride!"

"Stay!" she pleaded, tearfully,
"Dearest, let me go with thee!"
But his lip, as hers it met
Whispered tenderly — "Not yet!"

Paler grew his beaming face
As he gave the last embrace,
And the pallid shadow fell
On the brow he loved so well.

Then with loving fingers fair
Smoothed she back his dewy hair,
Whispering — "Across the sea,
Soon, beloved, I follow thee!"

They were parted; silently
Moved the boat across the sea,
While the youth, across the tide
Beckoned to his waiting bride.

Listening and waiting there
Slowly she unbound her hair,
And from out its sunny curls
Shook the flowers and stringéd pearls.

Slowly passed the hours away
As she sat beneath the spray,
Singing soft a mournful note,
Waiting the returning boat.

Soon it floated to her feet,
And her voice was yet more sweet
As she sung triumphantly,
"Now, beloved, I come to thee!"

Slowly from the crumbling shore,
Moved the boat as once before,
And her voice, the waves along
Changed into an angel's song;

As the mist forever more
Shrouding all the other shore
Parted clearly to my view
And the spirit-boat went through,

Melting softly from my sight
In a flood of living light,
And upon the other side
Met the bridegroom and his bride.

TO-DAY.

A STAR whose radiance far and bright
  Has shone till now along my way,
Is gathering up its robe of light,
  And fading from my sight — to-day.

A hand that I had prayed to clasp
  In mine, through life's uncertain way,
Is falling coldly from my grasp
  And leaving me alone, — to-day.

A hope that brightened summer's morns,
  Fades, with this autumn eve, away, —
The path I tread has more of thorns
  And fewer blossoms, from to-day.

I weep not o'er my buried trust;
  I have no pleading word to say; —
I lay my forehead in the dust
  And pray for patient strength — to-day!

IMPARTIALITY.

My window reaches the cottage eaves,
And o'er it an elm with drooping leaves
Its light and graceful drapery weaves,
With shadow and light uncertain;—
And a robin brown, with a bright red vest
Covering all her musical breast,
Has woven a soft and cosy nest
In the folds of the leafy curtain.

I love to sit by the window here
And watch her bringing the dainty cheer,
Crumbs, bugs, and worms, to her birdlings dear
Whose appetites shock calculation;
But of all the bugs I have seen her get,
In storm or calm, dry weather or wet,
She never has brought them a humbug yet—
I honor her penetration!

To meet her coming, a tiny head
That seems all mouth, pops up from its bed,
And ere the gaping thing is fed,
  Another, and yet another;
And then, with strict exactitude
She weighs and divides the precious food,
Giving part to each of her hungry brood, —
  A just, impartial mother!

I wish Dame Fortune, who goes her way
Over the wide world, day by day,
Dispensing as sheer caprice may say,
  The gifts which are hers to scatter, —
Sowing them broadcast, devoid of rule,
And in a manner provokingly cool,
Giving always some knave or fool
  By far the best of the matter;

Giving fame to one, and wealth to two,
And happiness to a blessèd few,
And nothing to me, and ditto to you,
  In such a partial fashion, —
Would come to the window here with me,
And watch the nest in the swinging tree,
And learn of the mother-bird to be
  More just in her distribution!

BOTH SIDES OF THE QUESTION.

THE SIDE APPARENT.

Ah, dearest, I have loved you long and well,
  Your lovely face to me perfection seems,
Your gentle voice, a musical underswell,
  Mingles all sweetly with my tide of dreams ; —
Say, will you make my home a paradise ?
  Be Eve within my Eden, dearest one ?
Should sorrow come, I'll kiss from your soft eyes
  The tears, and grieve because *you* grieve, my own !
Our lives shall pass like the sweet days of June,
  Full of bright blossoms and bird-melody,
Love in our hearts shall sing its sweetest tune,
  And every throb repeat its harmony !
Yes, dearest ! be my own, my worshipped wife !
Your love shall be my bliss, — your happiness, my life !

THE SIDE TRANSPARENT.

Dearest! resign this life of careless joy
For the stern duties of a married life!
Leave books and songs for practical employ,
And be, in all respects, a pattern wife!
Consent your every girlish taste to doff, —
To practice sweeping floors and making pies,
To sew on buttons ere their coming off,
And come what may, meet me with smiling eyes!
And more, — agree to yield up every friend,
Excepting such as I shall signify,
To stay indoors from year's end to year's end,
And never think yourself abused thereby!
In short, my dear, by uttering one sweet word,
Make me, your humblest slave, *your master and your lord!*

THE LIVING.

I WEEP no longer for the dead,
My tears are for the living shed,—
The living, whose o'erwearied feet
A dark and thorny pathway beat,—
The living, who in shame and sin,
Eclipse the light that might have been;
The living, who so wildly crave
The tearless quiet of the grave!

I weep for thee, oh, erring one,
Whose deeds of good are all undone,—
Whom all love's strivings could not win
Back from the paths of guilt and sin;
Thou who hast wronged a true heart's trust,
And trod it, bleeding, in the dust,—
Oh, lost to truth and purity
I weep for thee,—I weep for thee!

I weep for thee, oh, suffering heart,
Whose fate can know no brighter part,—
Left to the darkness of despair,
And tried beyond its strength to bear;
Breaking because it may not yield,
Bruised by the hand that should have healed,—
Scorned, slighted, crushed so cruelly,—
I weep for thee,—I weep for thee!

I weep for thee, oh fair young child,
Thrown on a world so wide and wild,—
Doomed, for another's sin, to stray
Along life's darkest, weariest way;—
Born to no heritage but tears,
And toil, and pain, through all life's years,—
Oh, heir of grief and poverty,
I weep for thee,—I weep for thee!

I weep no longer for the dead;—
The wind sings sweetly o'er their bed
A soothing hymn—a lulling tune,—
They sleep—they *rest*,—oh, blessèd boon!
Better that those for whom I weep
Were lying in their graves asleep!
Oh, no!—I weep not for the *dead*,—
My tears are for the *living* shed!

LET ME IN.

WHEN the summer evening's shadows
  Veiled the earth's calm bosom o'er,
Came a young child, faint and weary,
  Tapping at a cottage door;
"Wandering through the winding wood-paths
  My worn feet too long have been;
Let me in, oh, gentle mother,
      Let me in!"

Years passed on; his eager spirit
  Gladly watched the flying hours;
"I am tired of childish trifling,
  I am tired of birds and flowers;
I will seek the bands of pleasure,
  I will join their merry din;
Let me in to joy and gladness,
      Let me in!"

Years sped on; yet vainly yearning
  Murmured still the restless heart;
"I am tired of heartless folly,
  Let the glittering cheat depart;

I have found in worldly pleasure
  Nought to happiness akin;
Let me in to love's warm presence,
      Let me in!"

Years flew on; a youth no longer
  Still he owned the restless heart;
"I am tired of love's soft durance,
  Sweet-voiced charmer, we must part!
I will gain a laurel chaplet,
  And a world's applause will win;
Let me in to fame and glory,
      Let me in!"

Years fled on; the restless spirit
  Never found the bliss it sought;
Answered hopes and granted blessings
  Only new aspirings brought;
"I am tired of earth's vain glory,
  I am tired of grief and sin;
Let me in to rest eternal,
      Let me in!"

Thus the unquiet yearning spirit,
  Haunted by a vague unrest,
Knocks and calls at every gateway,
  In a vain and endless quest;
Ever striving some new blessing
  Some new happiness to win,—
At some portal ever saying,
      "Let me in!"

TO AN IDEAL.

I SIT within my chamber's quiet stillness,
  Thinking sweet thoughts, dreaming sweet dreams of thee,
Caring not for the darkness or the chillness,—
  Thy fervent love is light and warmth to me!

The river rolls in waves of starrys plendor,
  Following its shining pathway to the sea,
Now silent, now with song subdued and tender,
  As flows the tide of my deep love to thee.

I love thee! never have the words been spoken
  By mortal lips, with such a passionate thrill,
The tie that binds our hearts can ne'er be broken,
  The harp love's hand hath swept will ne'er be still!

The soiling dust that dims earth's brightest splendor,
  Clouds not the stars, which far above it shine,
So time and change, through dimming love less tender,
  Reach not to the pure heaven of thine and mine!

Thy thrilling kiss upon my lips is lying,
  Thy clasping arm is still around me thrown,
While thy dear voice falls like a prophesying
  Upon my heart, — " My best beloved — my own ! "

I have enough of bliss ; — my full heart trembles
  Like a bowed lily over-brimmed with dew,
Or haply in its deep delight resembles
  A day-star drowning in the morning's blue

OF ONE BELOVED.

The one whom we have loved has passed along
The valley of the shadow; even now
Faith hears the echo of her angel-song,
And sees the crown of light upon her brow.

Why call the valley dark? — No shadowing
Of grief or gloom on her fair brow has place, —
Death's gentle angel with his snowy wing
Has swept all pain and sorrow from her face.

Why call the valley dark? it is that we
Look on it through a veil of grief the while?
It was not dark to her, — it could not be
When lighted by Our Father's loving smile.

Not dark to her; while those she held most dear,
Wept hopelessly, with tearful eyes cast down,
Her lifted eyes, with faith undimmed and clear,
Beheld afar the triumph and the crown!

Their eyes are tearful — hers have ceased to weep: —
  Their hearts are aching; — hers will ache no more;
For she hath crossed death's ocean, chill and deep,
  And found a welcome on the other shore.

As star-beams faint in morning light away,
  So softly have life's weary wings been furled,
And as I gaze, the pale lips seem to say,
  Though motionless — "At peace with all the world!

I know that when around the lighted hearth
  Ye gather, as the evening hours come on,
Like a soft cloud between your hearts and mirth
  Will come the memory of the absent one.

I know that ye will watch "the vacant chair,"
  And gazing dimly through your gathering tears
Will think of her who from her station there,
  Looked love upon you, for so many years.

But by the faith which is a joy to me,
  Cheering me on my way of grief and ill,
I know the one ye mourn so bitterly
  Though all unseen, will be among you still.

Unseen — yet will she comfort you, and bless, —
  Her gentle spirit, to its mission true,
Will love and cheer and guide you none the less
  Because her form is hidden from your view.

Let this sweet solace with your grieving blend,
And give your aching bosoms hope and peace ; —
Though you have lost your dearest earthly friend,
Lo, ye have gained an angel in her place !

ALMOST AN ANGEL.

I CANNOT say she hath an angel's face, —
I never saw an angel ; but it seems
She is akin to those bright forms of grace
Which sometimes mingle in our holiest dreams,
There is no worldliness in those soft eyes
Whose radiance might all other orbs eclipse, —
No trace of passion on the fair brow lies,
No evil line around the sweet red lips.
The pure cheek never hath had cause to blush,
Therefore 't is hueless as a lily leaf,
Save when across its snow, a sudden flush
Flits, as she speaks, with coloring faint and brief,
Ah ! there's enough of angelhood in thee
To make a heaven on earth for some one, — but — *not me !*

THE BROKEN HOME.

We were three — a happy circle, bound by strong and holy ties,
Father, mother, and a cherub just descended from the skies, —
With a heart as yet undarkened by one earthly stain or trace,
And the brightness of the heaven it had left, upon its face.

We were three; and softly o'er us shone the morning light of hope,
And we saw bright scenes of gladness in the future sweetly ope;
Or if clouds obscured a moment the calm sunshine of our skies,
No dark shade of doubt or distance dimmed the light of loving eyes.

We were three, — but one has wandered far into a foreign land,
Lured away from love's sweet presence, and its fond detaining hand,
From a wealth of warm affection which in words may not be told,
By the mocking hope of riches, and the dazzling gleam of gold.

We were three; but sadly sundered is our little circle now,
Since we miss the tender meaning printed on that cherished brow;
Absent are the clasping fingers, and the loving eyes which smiled
With an earnest fond affection on the mother and her child.

We are two; — and when the darkness steals along the weary earth,
And the lonely heart most deeply feels its dreariness and dearth,
Bends the mother o'er her infant with a grief too deep to speak,
While warm tear-drops fall unbidden on its fair unconscious cheek.

Ah, dear wanderer, doth fancy never picture to thy mind
The solitude and sorrow of the lone one left behind?
Are earth's treasures to be counted all her tenderness above?
Is the shining gold atonement for the absence of her love?

Time hath smiled upon thine infant, and a sweet and nameless grace
Speaks in every new expression dawning o'er her dimpled face;—
Is the glitter of the treasure which around thee brightly lies,
Dearer than the loving radiance smiling in her soft brown eyes?

Hasten your slow weary motion, oh ye laggard wings of time!
Bring the absent wanderer swiftly, safely to his native clime,—
Re-united then, the burden of our joyful song shall be
Rising gratefully and gladly up to heaven—"We are three!"

THE PANTRY.

THIS is the pantry, — and from floor to ceiling
 Are ranged the plates and pans in piles and rows,
But from their polished sides no anthems pealing
 Startle the boarders from their morning doze.

Ah, what a sound of crashes and vibrations
 Will rise when Dinah, with her cupboard keys,
Comes down to make the breakfast preparation
 With jingling spoons and crockery symphonies!

I hear, even now, the infinite loud chorus,
 The rattling dishes and the whistling steam, —
The echoes of the breakfasts gone before us,
 Still lingering in the kitchen like a dream.

The bursting shell of lobsters wrenched asunder,
 The hissing stew-pan, and the clashing blade,
And with a sound more horrible than thunder,
 The stunning gong, when breakfast is arrayed.

It is, oh, cook, with such discordant noises,
  With such accursed instruments as these,
Thou drownest slumber's sweet and kindly voices,
  And jarrest the celestial harmonies!

If half the skill we lavish on our dinners,
  If half the time we pass in cookery's courts,
Were spent in spreading truth and saving sinners,
  There were no need of arsenals or forts.

The epicure's should be a name abhorred,
  And every butcher who should lift again
His arm to strike his victim, on his forehead,
  Should wear forever more the curse of Cain.

Down the long dining-room, with soft vibrations,
  The echoing sounds grow fainter and then cease,
And at each chamber-door, with gentle patience,
  A voice comes saying, "Breakfast, if you please!"

We go. No longer from the kitchen's portals
  The din of pans and kettles shakes the skies,
But, sweetest sounds on earth to hungry mortals,
  The melodies of knives and forks arise.

MY NAME,

"AFTER YOU HAVE TAKEN YOUR NEW NAME AMONG THE ANGELS."

In the land where I am going
  When my earthly life is o'er,
When the tired hands cease their striving
  And the tried heart aches no more —
In that land of light and beauty
  Where no shadow ever came
To o'ercloud the perfect glory, —
  What shall be my angel name?

When the spirits who await me
  Meet me at my entering in,
With what name of love and music
  Will their welcoming begin?
Not the one so dimmed with earth-stains,
  Linked with thoughts of grief and blame,—
No, — the name which mortals give me
  Will not be my angel name!

I have heard it all too often
  Uttered by unloving lips, —
Earthly cares and sins and sorrows
  Dim it with their dark eclipse; —
I shall change it like a garment
  When I leave this mortal frame,
And at Life's immortal baptism,
  I shall have another name!

For the angels will not call me
  By the name I bear on earth,
They will speak a holier language
  Where I have my holier birth,
Syllabled in heavenly music
  Sweeter far than earth may claim,
Very gentle, pure and tender, —
  Such will be my angel name.

It has thrilled my spirit often
  In the holiest of my dreams,
But its beauty lingers with me
  Only till the morning beams.
Weary of the jarring discord
  Which the lips of mortals frame,
When shall I, with joy and rapture,
  Answer to my angel name?

YOU AND ME.

I WISH, dear love, we had a world,
  A world that's all our own,
Not large enough for wealth and power,
  But just for us alone;
A fairy island far away
  In some bright southern sea,
Where skies should shine and earth should smile
  Only for you and me, dear love,
    Only for you and me!

We'd have a pretty little cot
  With swallows in the eaves,
Where humming-birds glance in and out
  Among the whispering leaves,
A home of music, love and mirth
  With brook and bird and bee,
And birds should sing and bees should hum
  Only for you and me, dear love,
    Only for you and me!

A woodbine with caressing arms
  Should cling about our door,
And sweet wild-roses on the air
  Their fragrant breath should pour;
The sun should shine, the streams should sing,
  The flowers bloom gorgeously,
And all should shine and sing and bloom
  Only for you and me, dear love,
    Only for you and me!

A living fountain near our home
  Should make us music rare,
The sparkles of its shining spray
  Cooling the fragrant air;
We 'd listen oft in summer eves
  Its ringing melody,
Rejoicing that it leaped and sang
  Only for you and me, dear love,
    Only for you and me!

And when our lives had flowed along
  To three-score years and ten,
The length of days the Father good
  Giveth the sons of men, —
One in our death, as one in life,
  Our mingled hearts should be,
For death should come, if come he must,
  At once to you and me, dear love,
    At once to you and me!

The bosom thou hadst leaned upon
So trustingly in life,
Should be thy pillow ev'n in death,
My own belovéd wife!
We 'd rest within one quiet grave
Beside the murmuring sea, —
A grave just wide and deep enough
Only for you and me, dear love,
Only for you and me!

OUR AUTUMN.

THE voice of Nature singing mournful dirges
For the departing year,
Like the loud swelling of the ocean's surges,
Falls sadly on my ear.

October's smile the reddening hill is flushing
With transient loveliness,
And rosily the forest-trees are blushing
Beneath the frost's rude kiss.

Blossoms and bees and song-birds have departed
From this, our northern land,
And dark November, chill and icy-hearted,
Asserts her stern command.

In warmer climes, the smiling sun is shedding
A flood of summer beams,
And gorgeous flowers their brilliant leaves are spreading.
By ever-tinkling streams.

OUR AUTUMN.

There sylvan groves are fadelessly revealing
        A wilderness of bloom,
Loading the breeze, amid their shadows stealing,
        With exquisite perfume.

Yet does our northern winter have a mission
        To these warm hearts of ours,
Richer than all the blooming and fruition
        Flushing the land of flowers.

It gathers up the gems of tender feeling
        Forgot in summer's mirth,
And scatters them, with soft and bright revealing,
        Around the social hearth.

So, while without are winds and boisterous weather,
        Yet, safe in home's repose,
Our northern hearts beat lovingly together,
        Through all the time of snows.

Therefore the voice of Nature, singing dirges
        For the departing year,
Like the loud swelling of the ocean's surges,
        Is music to my ear.

MY BABIES.

Twin blossoms in a field of single flowers
Like, yet unlike; — each lovely in itself,
Yet borrowing beauty of its counterpart, —
Such were my babies when I looked on them,
And thus I dream of them,—close linked with thoughts
Of doves, lambs, lilies, and all innocent things.

Lucy had laughing eyes, which danced and shone,
Brimming with baby mirth and playfulness, —
And her sweet voice was round and musical
As a young robin's warble, when he first
Learns the full value of the gift of song,
And, swinging on a spray of trembling leaves,
Rocked softly by the sportive morning wind, —
With dewy wing half spread and quivering,
Opens his golden throat, and seems to fling
His soul into his music; — and her laugh,
A baby's laugh, — the gladdest sound on earth,

Was full of summer melody and glee
As the clear tinkle of a rain-born brook
Flowing along among loose pebble-stones,
And through long grass, and over drowning flowers.
Methought her heart was of those happy ones
Elastic, glad and hopeful, — formed to see
Only the sparkles on the cup of life,
Unmindful of the bitter dregs below, —
To sing gay ballads and sweet loving songs,
Which leave no mournful echo in the soul.

Lizzie was slight and delicate; in her eyes
There shone a light like star-shine after rain,
Dewy and deep and tender; from their depths
Looked out the soul of woman, even then, —
Full of a sweet yet mournful prophecy,
Radiant with smiles, yet ripe for raining tears.
And when she smiled, the dimples came and danced
And deepened in her cheek, and round her lips,
Like whirlpools in deep water. As I gazed
It seemed to me that hers was one of those
Earnest yet delicate natures, — finely turned, —
Fragile, yet strong to suffer and endure, —
Timid and sensitive, and yet sublime
In their impassioned deep intensity, —
Such as God leads through dark and weary ways,
Making them perfect through much suffering.

Here, as has been my habit, I have called
These sweet twin-children *mine;* but though my soul
Yearns towards them with a love and tenderness
Such as to aching fills a mother's heart,
Thrilling it with a deep delicious pain, —
For her first-born, — still, they are not mine own; —
God gave them to another, — who will smile
And pardon me that my full heart speaks out
And calls them my dear babies, — for they are
By love's sweet spirit of adoption, mine.
She will forgive me, too, if in my dreams,
Lizzie's soft eyes smile oftenest back to mine,
And Lizzie's head lies oftenest on my breast.
Her own heart tells her why, like him of old,
I love not one *less*, but the other *more!*

God bless my babies! I could almost weep
That when they shall have grown to womanhood
Their hearts will shrine no memory of her
Who held them on her bosom for a day
And then departed. This is selfish, weak, —
I will not stain my blessing with these tears; —
Mayhap my arms will circle them again,
And mayhap, never. Let it be or no;
God bless my babies!

A BRACE OF SONNETS.

I.

I'VE noted oft, and not without surprise
  How true it is of each and every one,
That beauty dwelleth in the gazer's eyes
  Rather than in the features gazed upon.
Now there's an impassioned swain across the street
  Who sees such beauty in his Susan Jane, —
A dumpy damsel whom I often meet,
  With freckled face, red curls, and speech ungain,
As charmed the painters of the olden time,
  The grand old masters of a former age,
Inspiring their rare pencillings sublime
  Till the mute canvas spoke; — and I'll engage
He dreams of angels harping heavenly strains,
And every angel's face and voice is Susan Jane's!

II.

Music is in the ear of him who hears,
As beauty in the eyes of him who sees;
I'll wager now, no "music of the spheres,"
No concert grand of nature's harmonies,
No sound of distant harp-notes on the wind,
No organ's loud reverberating swell,
No orchestra, nor voice of Jenny Lind,
Soundeth to Susan Jane one half so well
As that consumptive fiddle, which *he* keeps
In yonder attic, and sometimes o'nights
Thrums to her window-blind, and sings—"She sleeps,"
With an ear-torturing chorus, that affrights
All within hearing. Falsehood joined to crime!
He *knows* she's wide awake, and listening all the time!

EVELYN.

Stars looked softly from the heaven, — fireflies glimmered in the grass,—
Brightly down the moonlit river did the golden ripples pass
On that lovely night in summer, when my heart to yours, alas,
Told its love-tale, Evelyn!

I was stern, ambitious, worldly, — rugged as a mountain pine,
You were fragile, sweet and loving, — like a fond and clinging vine ; —
You were all too finely moulded for a nature such as mine,—
Time has proved it, Evelyn!

As a rude child plucks a lily, whose sweet life has just begun,
Crushing it unkindly, heedless of the treasure he has won,
Till the fragile blossom withers, — perishes as you have done,
Thus I won you, Evelyn!

Ah, there never shone a morning half so lovely and divine
As the one which saw us standing at the altar's sacred shrine,
When I listened half-enraptured, as your sweet lips uttered, "Thine
And forever!" Evelyn!

Oh, it seems but yester morning that I saw you standing there,
While your pure heart's bashful throbbings shook the white buds in your hair,
And amid your loose curls gleaming rose your shoulders pale and fair, —
You were lovely, Evelyn!

But I wronged your fond affection and your high heart's holy trust, —
Left your heart, a harp neglected, till its strings grew dim with rust, —
Brought your fair head's golden tresses down in sorrow to the dust,
I who loved you, Evelyn!

Yes, I loved you, — but my spirit could not to your own aspire, —
Mine was of the world, and worldly; — yours, a gleam of heavenly fire; —
I gave earthly love and blessing, — but you longed for something higher,
Which I had not, Evelyn!

Never on your tender beauty blew a blast too cold or
rude, —
Yours was all that wealth could purchase, — yours was
every earthly good,
Dainty fare, rich gems and garments, — but your spirit
pined for food,
And I starved it, Evelyn!

I remember all your kindness, all your patience mild and
meek,
How a word or look unloving brought the color to your
cheek,
But you never chid or blamed me, though ungently I might
speak, —
Dear, forgiving Evelyn!

It was in the sweet October, when the earth was paved
with gold,
When the days were warm and rosy, and the nights were
chill and cold,
As the banner of the sunset was above the hills unrolled,
That you left me, Evelyn!

Unseen spirits circled round you, singing soft seraphic
psalms,
Unseen wings about you waving, fanned you with elysian
balms, —
I was very near to heaven, when within my clasping arms,
You lay dying, Evelyn!

From my neck your arm fell slowly, failing from its light
embrace, —
Drooped your sunny lashes softly, — faded life's last rosy
trace, —
And the bright waves of your tresses flowed around a
still pale face, —
You were dead, my Evelyn!

But they said you lived with angels, — darling, did they
tell me true?
Tell me, are your sister-angels bright and beautiful as you?
Do they love you, my adored one, better than I used to do?
No, they can not, Evelyn!

Does the memory of sorrow reach beyond this clouded
sphere?
Does your pure heart still remember all the pain it suf-
fered here?
Do you look upon me kindly, in my anguish lone and
drear?
Do you love me, Evelyn?

Tell me, is the love of angels like the love which mortals
know?
Do you tell them mournful stories of your earthly long
ago? —
Do they ever bring you tidings of the lone one left below? —
Do they call you "Evelyn?"

Though your face so sweet and gentle underneath the
grass-blooms lies,
Silent, lifeless, unreproving,— yet your spirit never dies,—
Wheresoever I may wander, still your sad rebuking eyes
Come and haunt me, Evelyn !

Ah, a dark fate is upon me, since I wronged your gentle
trust, —
Life's best joys, like Dead Sea apples, on my lips have
turned to dust, —
Fearfully are you avengèd,— but my punishment is just,—
I have earned it, Evelyn !

Yet not long shall be our parting : with a thrill of joy
divine,
I recall the blest assurance which your dear eyes gave to
mine,
On that happy bridal morning as your sweet lips uttered,
"Thine,
And *forever !*" Evelyn !

THE AWAKENING.

Cradled soft by his snowy wings,
  Love lay sleeping, one summer day,
Arrows and bows were forgotten things,
  As wrapped in his blissful dreams he lay, —
When gentle Merit came wandering by,
  With drooping lashes and humble heart; —
And Love, as he slumbered, caught her eye, —
  So, brushing the curtaining leaves apart,

She kissed his fair forehead and whispered "Rise!
  Heedest thou, Love, who is calling thee?"
But Love half-opened his drowsy eyes,
  And shook his white shoulders angrily,
While Merit, with sighs and a saddened look,
  Reclosed the branches his rest above,
And wrote in her heart's tear-spotted book, —
  "Merit may never waken Love!"

Soon, Beauty came, with her form of grace.
  Her faultless features and queenly air,
And bending over the young boy's face,
  She smiled as she saw him sleeping there;
And Love sprang up from his rosy rest,
  And shaking his wings with wild delight.
He fondly clasped to his gladdened breast
  The radiant maiden who charmed his sight.

But Merit, retired from Love apart,
  While to hide her gushing tears she strove,
Had seen, with an almost breaking heart
  How easily Beauty awakened Love, —
And she turned away, with the hopeless look
  So sad to see in the eye of youth,
And wrote in her heart's half-opened book.
  Tearfully, sadly, this bitter truth: —

"Alas, with Love it is ever so —
  All vainly may *Merit* shake him,
But one careless glance let *Beauty* throw,
  And how strangely soon 't will wake him!"

IN VAIN.

HEAVILY the winter rain
Plashes on the broken pane, —
On the hearth the embers die,
And the night-wind, fitfully
Entering at the shattered door,
Blows the ashes round the floor,
While in mortal strife with pain
Lies she who has lived in vain.

She was fated. As a child
No fond love upon her smiled,
For the hand that would have been
Strong to shield from woe and sin,
And the eyes whose loving light
Would have led her steps aright,
Since her birth in dust have lain, —
Therefore hath she lived in vain.
Harsh reproof and unkind words
Jarred her spirit's tender chords, —

Angry glance and threatening frown
Darkened childhood's gladness down,—
Nothing gentle, kind or good
Smiled upon her womanhood,—
Burdened sore were heart and brain,—
Is it strange she lived in vain?

Love came with his angel air,
Breathing vows as false as fair,—
And his wreath with promise rife
Crowned her as a worshipped wife,—
But the heart she trusted in
Turned aside to guilt and sin,
Leaving on her life their stain—
Wonder not she lived in vain!

Grief and poverty and care
Marred her face, once young and fair,—
Toil and want and sorrow's storm
Bowed her head and bent her form,
And her heart, a hopeless bark,
Drifted through life's tempest dark,
Till at last, in want and pain,
Dies she who has lived in vain.

No one cares that thus she dies;
No fond friend with tearful eyes
O'er her pillow hovereth,
Watching her uneven breath,

Holding her pale purpling hand,
Counting life's last wasting sand.
Mourn her requiem, wailing rain!
She is dead who lived in vain!

Life has been all dark and chill, —
Let her rest be dim and still;
Lay her in a shadowed glade
Where no sunbeam ever strayed, —
Place, mayhap, a simple stone
By her grave so sadly lone, —
Trace thereon in letters plain,
"Here she lies who lived in vain!"

STREET MUSIC.

METHOUGHT a sweet sound from the street uprose, —
  And as I pause, and strive again to hear,
"St. Patrick's Day" draws softly to its close,
  And "Jordan's" waves flow sweetly to my ear,
What though from humble source the chorus floats?
  Music is music, and I listen still;
I have "an ear," — ay, *two!* — Even jews-harp notes
  Pass current with me, hear them where I will,
A slight Italian boy, with jetty hair
  Shading dark eyes, grinds out the melody,
Pulverized music! — In his garb and air
  I read of sunnier lands beyond the sea,
And, dreaming, wander to a fairer clime,
Recalled, too suddenly, by — "*If you please, a dime!*"

THE APRIL BREEZE.

Soft breeze, with breath so cool and sweet,
   Herald of spring's bright gladsomeness,
With joy I lift my face to meet
   Once more thy light and bashful kiss.

Earth's unawakened bosom yields
   No odor to perfume thy wing,
For scarcely o'er the snowy fields,
   Has breathed the first warm sigh of Spring.

The woods are lone and leafless yet,
   No blossom sends its incense up,
Not even one sweet violet
   Has dared to lift its azure cup.

Not even the snow-drop blossometh,
   Awakened by the early showers,
Yet something in thy soft rich breath
   Speaks sweetly of the unborn flowers.

It may be that thy tell-tale tone
  Predicts how soon the buds will start,
Or, whispering of spring-times gone,
  Recalls their fragrance to my heart.

Welcome thy breath so soft and sweet,
  Herald of spring's bright gladsomeness!
With joy I lift my face to meet
  Once more thy light and bashful kiss!

PICTURES OF MEMORY.

AMONG the beautiful dresses
  Which hang on the wardrobe wall,
There is one of simple muslin
  That seemeth the best of all;
Not for the waist's trim fitting,
  Not for the sleeves' full flow,
Not for the neat little figures
  Which sprinkle the skirt below,—
Not for its pretty pattern
  Of roses under a hedge,
Not for its graceful flounces
  With nicely embroidered edge,—
Not for the folds on the boddice
  Where the satin buttons rest,
Nor the lace, nor the bows of ribbon,
  It seemeth to me the best.

I once had a darling sister
With eyes that were dark and deep,
And hers was this dress of muslin
Which sacredly now I keep.
Light as the down that dances
Where the dandelions grow,
We roved through our happy childhood,
The summers of long ago,
Till she stood at the marriage altar
On one of the autumn eves,
In a robe of embroidered satin
With very extensive sleeves.

Sweetly her white arms folded
My neck in a meek embrace,
As the snowy veil of the bridal
Silently covered her face.
Oh, my heart has been very lonely,
And our home has lost its light,
Since she fell, in her saint-like beauty,
In love with that college wight!
Therefore of all the dresses
Thet hang on the wardrobe wall,
The one of simple muslin
Seemeth the best of all!

LOST AND SAVED.

Darkly falls the stormy even,
Fiercely frowns the angry heaven,
While the bitter wind is calling,
And the driving sleet is falling.

Homeless, parentless and lonely,
Cared for by the angels only,
Roams a child, unblest by pity,
Through the mazes of the city.

No kind father's eye beholds her;—
No fond mother's love enfolds her,
And when evening shadows gather
Teaches her to say "Our Father!"

Round her neck, with soft caresses,
Cling her wild neglected tresses,—
Hail and snow, with glittering spangles
Gemming all their golden tangles.

None to smoothe their wavy beauty, —
None to guide to right and duty, —
None to show her worldly favor,
None to love, and none to save her.

Lost, poor friendless child, forever,
Castaway on life's wild river, —
Lost! amid its wild commotion
Rushing down to sin's dark ocean!

Where a proud and stately dwelling
Is of wealth and splendor telling,
By fatigue and sleep o'ertaken,
Sinks at last, the poor forsaken.

On the marble steps reclining,
Pillowed by her tresses shining,
With the snow around her heaping,
Sinks she in her chilly sleeping.

Bright the eye of morning flashes,
Beaming from its jetty lashes, —
Still with weary head reclining
Sleeps the child with tresses shining.

O'er her form the snow hath drifted,
And among her loose locks sifted, —
Silent lies she, — white and frozen,
On the bed so blindly chosen.

Saved! from wretchedness and error—
Saved from guilt's remorseful terror,—
Saved from sorrow's weary wearing,—
Saved from hopeless, dark despairing.

"Saved!" the angel band are saying,—
"Saved from sinning—saved from straying,—
Gladly we the lost lamb gather
To the bosom of our Father!"

TO ONE INSPIRED.

Thou of the snowy heart
  Passionless — cold, —
Though my heart's love to thee
  Vainly was told,
Now for a lowlier boon
  Humbly it bends —
Though thou canst love me not
  Let us be friends!

Thou of the pure white brow
  Stainless and calm,
Though for thy heavenward heart
  Earth has no charm,
Still the fond prayer to thee
  Warmly ascends —
Though thou canst love me not
  Let us be friends!

Thou of the lofty soul
  Sinless and fair,
Though to thy love, my heart
  May not aspire,
Prayers for thy happiness
  Upward it sends, —
Craving but one sweet boon, —
  Let us be friends!

OVER THE WAY.

There's a cottage just over the way,
  Where, whenever my eyes I am raising,
They will always unconsciously stray,
  And never grow weary of gazing.
Such gentleness, sweetness and grace,
  Was never yet equalled, I'm certain,
As shines in the beautiful face
  Revealed by that wind-lifted curtain!

Oh, a sea-nymph might safely be proud
  Of the tresses that forehead adorning, —
With hue like a golden-tinged cloud
  Just seen in the dim of the morning.
Oh, that voice by a seraph was given,
  And that laugh has a musical tinkle
And those eyes have the color of heaven
  When the stars are beginning to twinkle!

And then such a gem of a nose
  All likeness and rivalry scorning,
And the lips like the heart of a rose
  Blown apart by the first breath of morning!
Oh, that cottage just over the street!
  How can I do other than love it?
For its inmate so lovely and sweet
  'Twere no sin for an angel to covet!

Such beauty! it dazzles the eye, —
  Oh, its owner is fairer than Venus!
But alas, I confess with a sigh,
  There's more than that curtain between us!
For memory comes with a start, —
  Ah, too long has its power been parried, —
For like ice to my love-smitten heart
  Comes the dread recollection — *she's married!*

FEBRUARY.

I LOVE New England's summer-times; I hold
Them dearer far than those of sunnier climes.
But while my fingers purple with the cold,
I can't in conscience, praise its winter-times!

I watch not now the gentle autumn rain,
I hear no more its soft monotonous song,
But silently upon my window pane,
The frost is painting pictures all night long.

A February morning; — pale and faint
The dawning light seems frozen in the sky.
While with the calm endurance of a saint
I raise my window-curtain shiveringly —

Raise it, but all in vain, — the envious frost
Forbids my gaze, though often I essay,
Till by my warm repeated breathings crossed,
Part of the fairy broidery melts away.

The village smokes rise through the keen blue air
Trembling and faint, as seeming half afraid;
I envy the untroubled sleepers there
Who lie and doze until the fires are made.

I know 't is late, — I cannot tell the hour, —
The cold has stopped the clock, and hushed its chime, —
Potent indeed must be the frost-king's power
To palsy thus the mighty hands of time!

Life's waking pulses throb more audibly
And mingled sounds of toil and bustle swell, —
I hear the greetings of the passers-by,
And the sharp summons of the breakfast-bell.

The day's loud strife and turmoil is begun;
A busy crowd flows through the noisy street, —
Horses stand shivering with their blankets on,
And crisp snow crackles under hurrying feet.

Children are hastening school-ward, brisk and gay,
Young laughing girls, and boyhood rude and bold,
While beauty trips along the sparkling way,
Her fair cheek reddened by the biting cold.

The day has gone at last, brief, blue and cold,
And evening shivers o'er the frozen earth; —
All who have homes, hie to their sheltering fold, —
Heaven pity those who have no home or hearth!

The fall of hoofs, the sound of hasty feet,
  Become less frequent as the light declines;
The wind blows bleakly down the lonely street,
  Where flickeringly the early lamp-light shines.

No longer by the sunshine gilded o'er,
  The village walls rise cold and bleak and bare,
The cattle shiver at the stable door,
  Their nostrils smoking in the bitter air.

There sounds no bird-song from the forest now,
  No music wakened by the evening's breath, —
No murmuring rustle of the wind-stirred bough,
  But all is silent as the sleep of death.

Winter has laid his hand on Nature's lip
  And she is silent, with obedience true,
And silently the new moon's silver tip
  Comes slanting keenly through the frosty blue.

The welcome dark shuts out the frigid dearth
  Of the white landscape, desolate and wild,
And night folds closely round the weary earth,
  Like a great blanket round a sleepy child.

TRUE LOVE CAN FORGET.

Has death or change in its course bereft you?
  Does life seem worthless and dark and vain?
You may say that one you have loved has left you,
  But not that you never shall love again!

I know you think that your heart's deep feeling
  Can never waver, nor change, nor dim,
That no new charm will be o'er it stealing,
  No new voice warble love's angel hymn!

A pleasing fable is "love undying,"
  And one which daily is proved untrue,
For with fallen idols around us lying
  We seek another, and love anew!

We love to think, when our best and dearest
  Are buried, our hearts are buried too,
That our love, which life has proved sincerest,
  In death's deep darkness will still be true,—

True, though its idol is coldly lying
  Under the grave-sods, beneath our tread,
Though the worshipped lips make no replying,
  And the heart once loving, lies still and dead.

We love to think we shall always cherish
  The thought of a buried form and face,
For 't is hard to own that when *we* shall perish,
  Some other idol will take our place!

We try to think that the hearts which love us,
  To which our own yield a sweet return,
Are steady and true as the stars above us,
  Which, though we die, will not cease to burn!

Yet wherefore cherish the fond believing?
  Can we love a handful of lifeless dust?
And our weak hearts, "*above all* deceiving,"
  Can they *always* cling to a buried trust?

No! the heart with an impulse kindly given,
  Craves *living* love, as a flower the sun,
And when one love from its clasp is riven,
  It *seeks another and still loves on!*

TOO LATE.

HAVE you seen a being fair
With sad eyes and golden hair,
And a more than mortal grace
Shining through her pale sweet face?

Have you seen her whom I seek?
Hers is beauty pure and meek,
Such as charms our wildered eyes
In our dreams of Paradise.

Rarest diamonds always shine
In the deepest, darkest mine,
Fairest blossoms have their birth
On the dreariest wastes of earth,—

Thus the angel-presence sweet
Sent to guide my wayward feet,
Was to me, in love and light,
As the star is to the night.

But as darkness hides from light,
As from day retreats the night,
So, with scornful heart the while,
Fled I from her loving smile.

She was fair — ay, very fair, —
Goldenly her shining hair
Round the pure white brow below
Fell, like sunlight over snow, —

Or like that soft glow that lies
Sometimes in the sunset skies,
Or the glory artists paint
Round the forehead of a saint.

Not the summer heaven's clear blue,
Not the violet's tender hue,
Nor the gloom of midnight skies
Can describe her glorious eyes.

When the twilight solemnly
Walks along the dreaming sea,
On its breast a shadow lies
Tinted like those haunting eyes.

Yet I loved her not; my soul
Scorned to own her sweet control,
And I fled o'er land and sea,
Only that she followed me!

Over ocean's heaving tides,
Over craggy mountain sides,
Over many a barren waste
That no human foot had traced, —

Wandered I, to hide away
From her soft and holy sway,
Fearing but the loving smile
In her pleading eyes the while.

My hard heart, unknowing then,
Angels walk on earth with men,
Hated her, and bitterly,
Only that she cared for me!

And I shunned her all above,
Only that she sought my love;
Blind, blind eyes, which could not trace
"Angel" in that pure sweet face!

Every morning as I went
Through the doorway of my tent,
She went sadly on the way
I had trodden yesterday.

One bright morn, as I uprose
From my dream-disturbed repose,
Every breeze the whisper bore
"Go! I follow thee no more!"

And a keen remorseful dart
Pierced and rent my startled heart.
And across the weary waste
Wildly did my footsteps haste,

Searching where her tender feet
Torn by ragged thorns, had beat,
And her stainéd footprints lay
Mute rebukes, along the way; —

To the place where grief-oppressed,
Weary of her thankless quest,
She, the slighted one, was found
Fainting, dying, on the ground.

"Thou hast come too late," she said,
As I raised her drooping head, —
With a flash of bright surprise
Breaking from her misty eyes.

"Wayward one, I need not tell
I have sought thee long and well,
Thy stern will and stubborn heart
Bade us live and die apart!

"Fare thee well! I go before, —
I shall follow thee no more!
This shall thy life's penance be, —
Henceforth thou shalt seek for me!

"Drain the cup of grief and tears
Which *my* lips have pressed for years:
If it seemeth bitter, think
'Even such I bade *her* drink!'"

Cried I, kneeling,—"Angel, stay!
Pass not from my tears away!
Grant me pardon for the wrong
Thou hast meekly borne so long!

"Let my life atonement be—
Henceforth let *me* live for thee!
Let my love, through coming time,
Wipe away my darkening crime!"

Gone!—and raised in sad surprise,
Did not my dim-seeing eyes
Catch the shining of her hair
Fading in the upper air?

Henceforth in a fruitless quest,
Tortured by a wild unrest,
Like a pilgrim old and blind
Seek I what I may not find.

Often, as I pass along,
Ask I of the busy throng,
"Has an angel passed this way?"
And they answer, smiling,—"Nay!"

But with sad and tearful eyes
Looking upward to the skies,
See I yet her shining hair
Mingling with the upper air.

And when life's long search is o'er
I shall meet her yet once more,
With a thrill of glad surprise
Breaking from her glorious eyes!

DESTINED.

I LEAVE my wreath half-twined; — its blossoms lie
  Unbound and withering, in the wayside dust,
Crushed by the rude feet of the passers by, —
  And gird me to fulfil a loftier trust.

I leave my Eden, — my enchanted land, —
  The pleasant ways which I have loved to tread,
And kneel while Duty's stern untrembling hand
  Places her thorny crown upon my head.

I leave my early hopes, my morning dreams,
  My high aspirings, all, all unfulfilled,
And follow Destiny's far guiding beams,
  With tearless eyes, and steady heart unchilled.

I leave thy grave, oh, best beloved one!
  The home to which my heart turns yearningly; —
The hope so long and fondly nursed is done,
  I shall not claim the vacant place by thee!

And yet I leave *thee* not; — thou art not dead
  To me, although thou sleepest cold and low, —
Thy love illumes the rugged way I tread,
  And thy dear voice hath softly bid me, — "Go!"

For thou art always with me; though unseen,
  I feel thy presence ever, — trustingly
On thee, in weakness and in woe I lean,
  Hearing the sweet words — "I am still with thee!"

I turn my lips from Love's detaining kiss,
  I break the grasp of Friendship's clasping hand,
And pleading words, and tones of tenderness
  Fall on my ear like rain on desert-sand.

I say no farewell word, — I drop no tear, —
  I tremble not, whatever doom may wait
Upon my future; — I but breathe one prayer,
  And go forth quietly to meet my fate.

THE DESERT FOUNTAIN.

DISTANT lies a torrid desert, where the sunbeams ever glow,
Where the red air hotly trembles, and the deadly simooms blow,
And long troops of men and camels wander wearily and slow.

Just beside the scorching pathway, trod by many a weary band,
Lies a fertile green oasis, beautiful as fairy-land,
Rising like an isle enchanted, from the desert sea of sand.

There a crystal fountain gushes purely from its mossy bed,
There the soft grass, springing freshly, is with fragrant blossoms spread,
And rich fruits hang ripe and heavy, from the branches overhead.

Many a weary way-worn pilgrim, toiling slowly on his way,
Hearing far the fountain's tinkle, as it leaps in joyous play,
Turns aside to taste its coolness, tarrying till another day.

Gratefully he quaffs the freshness of the ripples at his feet,
Gladly plucks the fruits depending where the laden branches meet,
Then reclines, refreshed and strengthened, in a slumber deep and sweet.

But though close beside the pathway lies the cool and sylvan grot,
Thousands, travel-worn and drooping, daily pass the pleasant spot,
Heeding not the fountain's murmur, — seeing not and hearing not.

Thus on life's wide cheerless desert, stretching far on every hand,
Gushes love's pure holy fountain, foretaste of a happier land,
Sending forth its blessed music far across the desert sand.

Many a fainting, heart-sick wanderer, toiling wearily along,
Hears its gentle invitation, and forgets all grief and wrong,
In the joy of its refreshing, and the music of its song.

But though ever sounds its singing, loud and silver-toned
and clear,
Like an angel's voice of welcome to the wanderers passing
near,
Yet it falls, unheard, unheeded, on full many a careless ear.

Turn aside, oh, weary pilgrim, with slow step and tearful
eye,
Rest thee by the gushing waters, till the burning hours
go by,—
Turn aside and taste the blessing, ere the holy fount be dry!

TO ONE DYING.

I KNOW thou art dying; thy cheek is bright
With the rosy hue of life's sunset ray,
And in thine eyes unearthly light
I see the dawn of immortal day.

I know thou art dying; — it seems to me
Thy face is an angel's, even now,
And gazing on thee, I almost see
A glory gathering about thy brow.

I know thou art dying; thy hand's light clasp
Grows more uncertain from day to day,
And when it falls from my longing grasp,
Thy feet will walk in the shining way.

I know it all; — but no tear-drops start, —
My heart beats calmly and joyfully,
For I know the summons which bids us part,
Will only bring thee more near to me!

The fervent love which my bosom warms
Has not been suffered to gladden thine,
For men's traditions and empty forms
Have hedged thy spirit away from mine, —

Another has pillowed thy glorious head,
Another has watched thy rest above,
Has lived in the light thy presence shed,
While only I was thy spirit-love.

And now, when clearly thy cloudless eyes
Are gazing farther than mine may see,
And earthly fetters and earthly ties
Are slowly falling away from thee, —

I joy to know that thy life of pain,
Thy term of bondage is nearly flown,
That death will sever thy galling chain,
And make thee wholly mine own — *mine own!*

The burdens and crosses which earth lays on
Will vanish at death's releasing touch,
And thou who always since life begun
Hast wept and sorrowed and suffered much,

Wilt rise from the fetters which bind thee here
As a freed bird flies from captivity,
And come unfearing, to bless and cheer
The heart that has waited so long for thee.

In that existence, thy patient love
    Will break the shackles it wears in this,
And I shall feel from the sphere above
    Belovéd, thy first betrothal kiss!

TRUTH AND POETRY.

Strange Truth and Poetry are enemies,
    Treading forever on each other's toes!
Strange rhymes are always made of that which is
    Too false or silly to be said in prose!
Now here's a sonnet by our village poet
    "Inscribed to Kate," in most romantic style,
Whereas, — and one with half an eye might know it,—
    He means Sophronia Tompkins, all the while.
He sings of "golden curls." If fiery tresses
    Had heat to match their hue, *her* hair would burn;—
He mentions "airy grace," — while she possesses
    A form as shapeless as an old-time churn,
Heavens! after this I never shall inquire
Why people always call the poet's song a LYRE!

www.ingramcontent.com/pod-product-compliance
Lightning Source LLC
LaVergne TN
LVHW011214110826
845150LV00006B/1426

* 9 7 8 1 4 2 5 5 1 7 1 2 0 *